Back to Basics: Stock Investing

by Paul Mladjenovic, CFP

Publisher's Acknowledgments

Senior Acquisitions Editor:
Tracy Boggier

Project Manager:
Chad R. Sievers

Compilation Editor:
Georgette Beatty

Production Editor:
Tamilmani Varadharaj

Cover Images: (magnifying glass)
© godfather744431/Getty Images,
(bars) © godfather744431/Getty
Images

Cover Design: Wiley

Back to Basics:
Stock Investing

Published by John Wiley & Sons, Inc.
111 River St.
Hoboken, NJ 07030-5774
http://www.wiley.com

For general information on our other products and services, please contact our Business Development
Department in the U.S. at 317-572-3205.

ISBN 978-1-119-47268-1 (pbk); ISBN 978-1-119-47287-2 (ePub); ISBN 978-1-119-47284-1 (ePDF)

Manufactured in the United States of America

F10005512 102318

Contents

1

Assessing Your Financial Situation and Goals

Stocks can be a great component of most wealth-building programs, but you must first do some homework on a topic that you should be very familiar with — yourself. That's right. Understanding your current financial situation and clearly defining your financial goals are the first steps in successful investing.

This chapter is undoubtedly one of the most important chapters in this book. At first, you may think it's a chapter more suitable for some general book on personal finance. Wrong: Unsuccessful investors' greatest weakness is not understanding their financial situations and how stocks fit in. Often, I counsel people to stay out of the stock market if they aren't prepared for the responsibilities of stock investing, such as regularly reviewing the financial statements and progress of the companies they invest in.

Investors should make stocks a part of their portfolios, but the operative word is *part*. You should let stocks take up only a *portion* of your money. A disciplined investor also has money in bank accounts, investment-grade bonds, precious metals, and other assets that offer growth or income opportunities. Diversification is the key to minimizing risk. (For more on risk, see Chapter 3.)

Prepare a Balance Sheet

No matter what you hope to accomplish with stock investing, the first step you should take is to figure out how much you own and how much you owe. To do this, prepare and review your personal balance sheet. A *balance sheet* is simply a list of your assets, your liabilities, and what each item is currently worth so you can arrive at your net worth. Your *net worth* is total assets minus total liabilities. Knowing your net worth is important to your future financial success.

Composing your balance sheet is simple. Pull out a pencil and a piece of paper. For the computer-savvy, a spreadsheet software program accomplishes the same task. Gather all your financial documents, such as bank and brokerage statements and other such paperwork; you need figures from these documents. Then follow the steps outlined in the following sections. Update your balance sheet at least once a year to monitor your financial progress (is your net worth going up or down?).

Step 1: Have an emergency fund

First, list cash on your balance sheet. Your goal is to have at least three to six months' worth of your gross living expenses in cash and cash equivalents. Three to six months' worth is usually enough to get you through the most common forms of financial disruption, such as losing your job.

If your monthly expenses (or *outgo*) are $2,000, for example, you should have at least $6,000, and closer to $12,000, in a secure, FDIC-insured, interest-bearing bank account (or another relatively safe, interest-bearing vehicle such as a money market fund). Consider this account an emergency fund, not an investment. Don't use this money to buy stocks.

Too many Americans don't have an emergency fund, meaning that they put themselves at risk. One of the biggest problems during this past decade was that savings were sinking to record lows while debt levels were reaching new heights.

_____

_____

_____

People then sold many stocks because they needed funds for paying bills and servicing debt.

Resist the urge to think of your investment in stocks as a savings account generating more than 20 percent per year. This is dangerous thinking. If your investments tank or if you lose your job, you'll have financial difficulty, and that will affect your stock portfolio (you may have to sell some stocks in your account just to get money to pay the bills). An emergency fund helps you through a temporary cash crunch.

Step 2: List your assets in decreasing order of liquidity

Liquidity refers to how quickly you can convert a particular *asset* (something you own that has value) into cash. If you know the liquidity of your assets, you have some options when you need cash to buy some stock (or pay some bills). All too often, people are short on cash and have too much wealth tied up in *illiquid* investments such as real estate. *Illiquid* is just a fancy way of saying that you don't have the immediate cash to meet a pressing need. Review your assets and take measures to ensure that enough of them are liquid (along with your illiquid assets).

_____

_____

_____

Listing your assets in order of liquidity on your balance sheet gives you an immediate picture of which assets you can quickly convert to cash and which ones you can't. If you need money *now,* you can see that cash in hand, your checking account, and your savings account are at the top of the list. The items last in order of liquidity become obvious; they're things like real estate and other assets that can take a long time to convert to cash.

Table 1-1 shows a typical list of assets in order of liquidity. Use it as a guide for making your own asset list.

Asset Item	Market Value	Annual Growth Rate %
Current assets		
Cash on hand and in checking	$150	
Bank savings accounts and certificates of deposit	$5,000	1%
Stocks	$2,000	11%
Mutual funds	$2,400	9%
Other assets (collectibles and so on)	$240	
Total current assets	**$9,790**	

Table 1-1: *Listing Personal Assets in Decreasing Order of Liquidity*

(continued)

Asset Item	Market Value	Annual Growth Rate %
Long-term assets		
Auto	$1,800	–10%
Residence	$150,000	5%
Real estate investment	$125,000	6%
Personal items (such as jewelry)	$4,000	
Total long-term assets	**$280,800**	
Total assets	**$290,590**	

Table 1-1 *(continued)*

Here's how to break down the information in Table 1-1:

- **The first column** describes the asset. You can quickly convert *current assets* to cash — they're more liquid; *long-term assets* have value, but you can't necessarily convert them to cash quickly — they aren't very liquid.

- **The second column** gives the current market value for that item. Keep in mind that this value isn't the purchase price or original value; it's the amount you'd realistically get if you sold the asset in the current market at that moment.

- **The third column** tells you how well that investment is doing compared to one year ago. If the percentage rate is 5 percent, that item is worth 5 percent more today than it was a year ago. You need to know how well all your assets are doing so you can adjust your assets for maximum growth or get rid of assets that are losing money. Keep assets that are doing well (and consider increasing your holdings in these assets), and scrutinize assets that are down in value to see whether they're candidates for removal. Perhaps you can sell them and reinvest the money elsewhere. In addition, the realized loss has tax benefits (see Chapter 10).

Figuring the annual growth rate (in the third column) as a percentage isn't difficult. Say that you buy 100 shares of the stock Gro-A-Lot Corp. (GAL), and its market value on December 31, 2016, is $50 per share for a total market value of $5,000 (100 shares multiplied by $50 per share). When you check its value on December 31, 2017, you find out that the stock is at $60 per share for a total market value of $6,000 (100 shares multiplied by $60). The annual growth rate is 20 percent. You calculate this percentage by taking the amount of the gain ($60 per share less $50 per share equals $10 gain per share), which is $1,000 (100 shares times the $10 gain), and dividing it by the value at the beginning of the time period ($5,000). In this case, you get 20 percent ($1,000 divided by $5,000).

- **The last line** lists the total for all the assets and their current market value.

Step 3: List your liabilities

Liabilities are simply the bills that you're obligated to pay. Whether it's a credit card bill or a mortgage payment, a liability is an amount of money you have to pay back eventually (usually with interest). If you don't keep track of your liabilities, you may end up thinking that you have more money than you really do.

Table 1-2 lists some common liabilities. Use it as a model when you list your own. You should list the liabilities according to how soon you need to pay them. Credit card balances tend to be short-term obligations, whereas mortgages are long-term.

Liabilities	Amount	Paying Rate %
Credit cards	$4,000	18%
Personal loans	$13,000	10%
Mortgage	$100,000	4%
Total liabilities	$117,000	

Table 1-2: *Listing Personal Liabilities*

Here's a summary of the information in Table 1-2:

- **The first column** names the type of debt. Don't forget to include student loans and auto loans.

- **The second column** shows the current value (or current balance) of your liabilities. List the most current balance to see where you stand with your creditors.

- **The third column** reflects how much interest you're paying for carrying that debt. This information is an important reminder about how debt can be a wealth zapper. Credit card debt can have an interest rate of 18 percent or more, and it isn't even tax-deductible. Using a credit card to make even a small purchase costs you if you don't pay off the balance each month. Within a year, a $50 sweater at 18 percent costs $59 when you add in the annual potential interest on the $50 you paid.

If you compare your liabilities in Table 1-2 and your personal assets in Table 1-1, you may find opportunities to reduce the amount you pay for interest. Say, for example, that you pay 18 percent on a credit card balance of $4,000 but also have a personal asset of $5,000 in a bank savings account that's earning 2 percent in interest. In that case, you may want to consider taking $4,000 out of the savings account to pay off the credit card balance. Doing so saves you $640; the $4,000 in the bank was earning only $80 (2 percent of $4,000), while you were paying $720 on the credit card balance (18 percent of $4,000).

If you can't pay off high-interest debt, at least look for ways to minimize the cost of carrying the debt. The most obvious ways include the following:

- **Replace high-interest cards with low-interest cards.** Many companies offer incentives to consumers, including signing up for cards with favorable rates (recently under 10 percent) that can be used to pay off high-interest cards (12 to 18 percent or higher).

- **Replace unsecured debt with secured debt.** Credit cards and personal loans are *unsecured* (you haven't put up any collateral or other asset to secure the debt); they have higher interest rates because this type of debt is considered riskier for the creditor. Sources of *secured debt* (such as home equity line accounts and brokerage accounts) provide you with a means to replace your high-interest debt with lower-interest debt. You get lower interest rates with secured debt because it's less risky for the creditor — the debt is backed up by collateral (your home or your stocks).

- **Replace variable-interest debt with fixed-interest debt.** If you can't lower your debt, at least make it fixed and predictable.

Make a diligent effort to control and reduce your debt; otherwise, the debt can become too burdensome. If you don't control it, you may have to sell your stocks just to stay liquid.

Step 4: Calculate your net worth

Your *net worth* is an indication of your total wealth. You can calculate your net worth with this basic equation: total assets (Table 1-1) less total liabilities (Table 1-2) equals net worth (net assets or net equity).

Table 1-3 shows this equation in action with a net worth of $173,590 — a very respectable number. For many investors, just being in a position where assets exceed liabilities (a positive net worth) is great news. Use Table 1-3 as a model to analyze your own financial situation. Your mission is to ensure that your net worth increases from year to year as you progress toward your financial goals (I discuss financial goals later in this chapter).

_____

_____

_____

Totals	Amounts ($)	Increase from Year Before
Total assets (from Table 1-1)	$290,590	+5%
Total liabilities (from Table 1-2)	($117,000)	–2%
Net worth (total assets less total liabilities)	$173,590	+3%

Table 1-3: *Figuring Your Personal Net Worth*

Step 5: Analyze your balance sheet

After you create a balance sheet to illustrate your current finances, take a close look at it and try to identify any changes you can make to increase your wealth. Sometimes, reaching your financial goals can be as simple as refocusing the items on your balance sheet (use Table 1-3 as a general guideline). Consider these points:

- **Is the money in your emergency (or rainy day) fund sitting in an ultrasafe account and earning the highest interest available?** Bank money market accounts or money market funds are recommended. The safest type of account is a U.S. Treasury money market fund. Banks are backed by the Federal Deposit Insurance Corporation (FDIC), while U.S. Treasury securities are backed by the "full faith and credit" of the federal government. Shop around for the best rates at sites such as www.bankrate.com, www.lendingtree.com, and www.lowermybills.com.

- **Can you replace depreciating assets with appreciating assets?** Say you have two stereo systems. Why not sell one and invest the proceeds? You may say, "But I bought that unit two years ago for $500, and if I sell it now, I'll get only $300." You need to decide what helps your financial situation more — a $500 item that keeps shrinking in value (a *depreciating asset*) or $300 that can grow in value when invested (an *appreciating asset*).

- **Can you replace low-yield investments with high-yield investments?** Maybe you have $5,000 in a bank certificate of deposit (CD) earning 3 percent. You can shop around for a better rate at another bank, but you can also seek alternatives that can offer a higher yield, such as U.S. savings bonds or short-term bond funds. Just keep in mind that if you already have a CD and you withdraw the funds before it matures, you may face a penalty (such as losing some interest).

- **Can you pay off any high-interest debt with funds from low-interest assets?** If, for example, you have $5,000 earning 2 percent in a taxable bank account and you have $2,500 on a credit card charging 18 percent (which is not tax-deductible), you may as well pay off the credit card balance and save on the interest.

- **If you're carrying debt, are you using that money for an investment return that's greater than the interest you're paying?** Carrying a loan with an interest rate of 8 percent is acceptable if that borrowed money is yielding more than 8 percent elsewhere. Suppose you have $6,000 in cash in a brokerage account. If you qualify, you can actually make a stock purchase greater than $6,000 by using *margin* (essentially a loan from the broker). You can buy $12,000 of stock using your $6,000 in cash, with the remainder financed by the broker. Of course, you pay interest on that margin loan. But what if the interest rate is 6 percent and the stock you're about to invest in has a dividend that yields 9 percent? In that case, the dividend can help you pay off the margin loan, and you keep the additional income. (For more on buying on margin, see Chapter 9.)

- **Can you sell any personal stuff for cash?** You can replace unproductive assets with cash from garage sales and auction websites.

_____

_____

_____

- **Can you use your home equity to pay off consumer debt?** Borrowing against your home has more favorable interest rates, and this interest is still tax-deductible.

  Note: Paying off consumer debt by using funds borrowed against your home is a great way to wipe the slate clean. What a relief to get rid of your credit card balances. Just don't turn around and run up the consumer debt again. You can get overburdened and experience financial ruin.

Fund Your Stock Program

Many investors can reallocate their investments and assets to get money for stock investing. *Reallocating* means selling some investments or other assets and reinvesting that money into something else (such as stocks). It boils down to deciding what investment or asset you can sell or liquidate. Generally, you want to consider those investments and assets that give you a low return on your money (or no return at all). If you have a complicated mix of investments and assets, you may want to consider reviewing your options with a financial planner. Reallocation is just part of the answer; your cash flow is the other part.

Ever wonder why there's so much month left at the end of the money? Consider your cash flow. Your *cash flow* refers to what money is coming in (income) and what money is being spent (outgo). The net result is either a positive cash flow or a negative cash flow, depending on your cash management skills. Maintaining a positive cash flow (more money coming in than going out) helps you increase your net worth. A negative cash flow depletes your wealth and wipes out your net worth if you don't turn it around immediately.

The following sections show you how to calculate and analyze your cash flow. The first step is to do a cash flow statement. With this statement, ask yourself three questions:

- **What money is coming in?** Jot down all sources of income. Calculate income for the month and then for the year. Include everything: salary, wages, interest, dividends, and so on.

- **What is your outgo?** Write down all the things that you spend money on. List all your expenses. If possible, categorize them as essential and nonessential. You can get an idea of all the expenses that you can reduce without affecting your lifestyle.

- **What's left?** If your income is greater than your outgo, you have money ready and available for stock investing.

If your outgo is greater than your income, sharpen your pencil. Cut nonessential spending and/or increase your income. If your budget is tight, hold off on stock investing until your cash flow improves.

Step 1: Tally up your income

Using Table 1-4 as a worksheet, list and calculate the money you have coming in. The first column describes the source of the money, the second column indicates the monthly amount from each respective source, and the last column indicates the amount projected for a full year. Include all income, such as wages, business income, dividends, interest income, and so on. Then project these amounts for a year (multiply by 12) and enter those amounts in the third column.

Item	Monthly $ Amount	Yearly $ Amount
Salary and wages		
Interest income and dividends		
Business net (after taxes) income		
Other income		
Total income		

Table 1-4: *Listing Your Income*

Your total income is the amount of money you have to work with. Don't spend more than this amount. Always be aware of and carefully manage your income.

Step 2: Add up your outgo

Using Table 1-5 as a worksheet, list and calculate the money that's going out. The first column describes the source of the expense, the second column indicates the monthly amount, and the third column shows the amount projected for a full year. Include all the money you spend: credit card and other debt payments; household expenses, such as food and utility bills; and nonessential expenses.

Item	Monthly $ Amount	Yearly $ Amount
Payroll taxes		
Rent or mortgage		
Utilities		
Food		
Clothing		
Insurance (medical, auto, homeowner, and so on)		
Telephone/Internet		

Table 1-5: *Listing Your Expenses (Outgo)*

Item	Monthly $ Amount	Yearly $ Amount
Real estate taxes		
Auto expenses		
Charity		
Recreation		
Credit card payments		
Loan payments		
Other		
Total outgo		

Payroll taxes is just a category in which to lump all the various taxes that the government takes out of your paycheck. Feel free to put each individual tax on its own line if you prefer. The important thing is creating a comprehensive list that's meaningful to you.

The outgo doesn't include items such as payments to a 401(k) plan and other savings vehicles. Yes, these items do impact your cash flow, but they're not expenses; the amounts that you invest (or your employer invests for you) are essentially assets that benefit your financial situation versus expenses that don't help you build wealth. To account for the

401(k), simply deduct it from the gross pay before you calculate the preceding worksheet (Table 1-5). If, for example, your gross pay is $2,000 and your 401(k) contribution is $300, then use $1,700 as your income figure.

Step 3: Create a cash flow statement

The next step is creating a cash flow statement so that you can see (all in one place) how your money moves — how much comes in and how much goes out and where it goes.

Plug the amount of your total income (from Table 1-4) and the amount of your total expenses (from Table 1-5) into the Table 1-6 worksheet to see your *cash flow.* Do you have positive cash flow — more coming in than going out — so that you can start investing in stocks (or other investments), or are expenses overpowering your income?

Watch your cash flow; keep your income growing and your expenses and debt as low as possible.

Item	Monthly $ Amount	Yearly $ Amount
Total income (from Table 1-4)		
Total outgo (from Table 1-5)		
Net inflow/outflow		

Table 1-6: *Looking at Your Cash Flow*

Step 4: Analyze your cash flow

Use your cash flow statement in Table 1-6 to identify sources of funds for your investment program. The more you can increase your income and decrease your outgo, the better. Scrutinize your data. Where can you improve the results? Here are some questions to ask yourself:

- How can you increase your income? Do you have hobbies or skills that can generate extra cash?
- Can you get more paid overtime at work? How about a promotion or a job change?
- Where can you cut expenses?
- Have you categorized your expenses as either "necessary" or "nonessential"?
- Can you lower your debt payments by refinancing or consolidating loans and credit card balances?
- Have you shopped around for lower insurance or telephone rates?
- Have you analyzed your tax withholdings in your paycheck to make sure that you're not overpaying your taxes (just to get your overpayment back next year as a refund)?

_____

_____

_____

Set Your Financial Goals

Consider stocks as tools for living, just like any other investment — no more, no less. You must consider stock investing as a means to an end. When people buy a computer, they don't (or shouldn't) think of buying a computer just to have a computer. People buy a computer because doing so helps them achieve a particular result, such as being more efficient in business or playing fun games.

Know the difference between long-term, intermediate-term, and short-term goals, and then set some of each (see Chapter 2 for more information):

- *Long-term goals* refer to projects or financial goals that need funding five or more years from now.
- *Intermediate-term goals* refer to financial goals that need funding two to five years from now.
- *Short-term goals* need funding less than two years from now.

Stocks, in general, are best suited for long-term goals such as these:

- Achieving financial independence (think retirement funding)
- Paying for future college costs
- Paying for any long-term expenditure or project

Some categories of stock (such as conservative or large cap) may be suitable for intermediate-term financial goals. If, for example, you'll retire four years from now, conservative stocks can be appropriate. If you're optimistic (or *bullish*) about the stock market and confident that stock prices will rise, go ahead and invest. However, if you're negative about the market (you're *bearish,* or you believe that stock prices will decline), you may want to wait until the economy starts to forge a clear path.

Stocks generally aren't suitable for short-term investing goals because stock prices can behave irrationally in a short period of time. Stocks fluctuate from day to day, so you don't know what the stock will be worth in the near future. You may end up with less money than you expected. For investors seeking to reliably accrue money for short-term needs, short-term bank certificates of deposit or money market funds are more appropriate.

In recent years, investors have sought quick, short-term profits by trading and speculating in stocks. It's very important for you to understand the differences among *investing,* *saving,* and *speculating.* Investors who don't know the difference tend to get burned. Here's some information to help you distinguish among these three actions:

- *Investing* **is the act of putting your current funds into securities or tangible assets for the purpose of gaining future appreciation, income, or both.** You need time, knowledge, and discipline to invest. The investment can fluctuate in price, but you've chosen it for long-term potential.

- *Saving* **is the safe accumulation of funds for a future use.** Savings don't fluctuate and are generally free of financial risk. The emphasis is on safety and liquidity.

- *Speculating* **is the financial world's equivalent of gambling.** An investor who speculates is seeking quick profits gained from short-term price movements in a particular asset or investment. In recent years, many folks have been trading stocks (buying and selling in the short term with frequency), which is in the realm of short-term speculating.

2

Common Approaches to Stock Investing

Stocks are tools you can use to build your wealth. When used wisely, they do a great job. But when improperly applied, they can lead to disaster. This chapter shows you how to choose the right types of investments based on your short-term, intermediate-term, and long-term financial goals. You also decide on your purpose for investing and your style of investing.

Match Stocks and Strategies with Your Goals

The key to success in the stock market is matching the right kind of stock with the right kind of investment situation. You have to choose the stock and the approach that match your goals. (Check out Chapter 1 for more on defining your financial goals.)

Stocks are a means to an end. Your job is to figure out what that end is — or, more important, when it is. Do you want to retire in 10 years or next year? Must you pay for your kid's college education next year or 18 years from now? The length of time you have before you need the money you hope to earn from stock investing determines what stocks you should buy. Table 2-1 gives you some guidelines for choosing the kind of stock best suited for the type of investor you are and the goals you have.

Type of Investor	Time Frame for Financial Goals	Type of Stock Most Suitable
Conservative (worries about risk)	Long term (more than 5 years)	Large cap stocks and mid cap stocks
Aggressive (high tolerance to risk)	Long term (more than 5 years)	Small cap stocks and mid cap stocks
Conservative (worries about risk)	Intermediate term (2 to 5 years)	Large cap stocks, preferably with dividends
Aggressive (high tolerance to risk)	Intermediate term (2 to 5 years)	Small cap stocks and mid cap stocks
Short term	1 to 2 years	Stocks are not suitable for the short term. Instead, look at vehicles such as savings accounts and money market funds.

Table 2-1: *Investor types, financial goals, and stock types*

Type of Investor	Time Frame for Financial Goals	Type of Stock Most Suitable
Very short term	Less than 1 year	You *can* invest in stocks for less than a year, but you're not really investing — you're either trading or short-term speculating. Instead, use savings accounts and money market funds.

Dividends are payments made to a stock owner (unlike *interest,* which is payment to a creditor). Dividends are a great form of income, and companies that issue dividends tend to have more stable stock prices as well. For more information, see the later section "Income investing."

Table 2-1 gives you general guidelines, but not everyone fits into a particular profile. Every investor has a unique situation, set of goals, and level of risk tolerance. The terms *large cap, mid cap,* and *small cap* refer to the size (or *market capitalization,* also known as *market cap*) of the company. All factors being equal, large companies are safer (less risky) than small companies.

Invest for the Future

Generally, the length of time you plan to invest in stocks can be short-term, intermediate-term, or long-term. The following sections outline what kinds of stocks are most appropriate for each term length.

The short term

Short term generally means one year or less, although some people extend the period to two years or less. Short-term investing isn't about making a quick buck on stock choices — it refers to when you may need the money.

Every person has short-term goals. Some are modest, such as setting aside money for a vacation next month. Other short-term goals are more ambitious, such as accruing funds for a down payment to purchase a new home within six months. Whatever the expense, you need cash soon. If this sounds like your situation, stay away from the stock market.

I get a kick out of market analysts on TV saying things like this: "At $25 a share, XYZ is a solid investment, and we feel that its stock should hit our target price of $40 within six to nine months." It may hit that target amount (or surpass it), or it may not. Most of the time, the stock doesn't reach the target price, and the investor is disappointed. The stock can even go down.

The reason that target prices are frequently missed is that it's difficult to figure out what millions of investors will do in the short term. The short term can be irrational because so many investors have so many reasons for buying and selling that it can be difficult to analyze. If you invest for an important short-term need, you can lose very important cash quicker than you think.

During the raging bull market of 2002–2007, investors watched as some high-profile stocks went up 20 to 50 percent in a matter of months. Of course, when the 2008–2009 bear market hit and those same stocks fell 50 to 85 percent, a savings account earning a measly interest rate suddenly didn't seem so bad.

Short-term stock investing is very unpredictable. Stocks — even the best ones — fluctuate in the short term. In a negative environment, they can be very volatile. No one can accurately predict the price movement (unless he has some inside information), so stocks are definitely inappropriate for any financial goal you need to reach within one year. Refer to Table 2-1 for suggestions about your short-term strategies.

The intermediate term

Intermediate term refers to the financial goals you plan to reach in two to five years. For example, if you want to accumulate funds to put money down for investment in real estate four years from now, some growth-oriented investments may be suitable. (Find out more about growth investing later in this chapter.)

Although some stocks *may* be appropriate for a two- or three-year period, not all stocks are good intermediate-term investments. Some stocks are fairly stable and hold their value well, such as the stock of large or established dividend-paying companies. Other stocks have prices that jump all over the place, such as those of untested companies that haven't been in existence long enough to develop a consistent track record.

 If you plan to invest in the stock market to meet intermediate-term goals, consider large, established companies or dividend-paying companies in industries that provide the necessities of life (like the food and beverage industry or electric utilities). They're especially well-suited for intermediate investment goals.

If the company is going strong, you can continue holding the stock indefinitely. The more time you give a well-positioned, profitable company's stock to grow, the better you'll do.

The long term

Stock investing is best suited for making money over a long period of time. Usually, when you measure stocks against other investments in terms of five to ten or more years, they excel. If you examine any ten-year period over the past 50 years, you see that stocks beat out other financial investments (such as bonds) in almost every period when measured by total return (taking into account reinvesting and compounding of capital gains and dividends).

Your work doesn't stop at deciding on a long-term investment. You still have to do your homework and choose stocks wisely, because even in good times, you can lose money if you invest in companies that go out of business.

Virtually any investor with a long-term perspective should add stocks to his investment portfolio. Whether you want to save for a young child's college fund or for future retirement

_____

_____

_____

goals, carefully selected stocks have proven to be a superior long-term investment.

Invest for a Purpose

You shouldn't invest in stocks unless you have a purpose that you understand, like investing for growth or income. Keep in mind that stocks are just a means to an end — figure out your desired end and then match the means. The following sections can help.

Growth investing

When investors want their money to grow, they look for investments that appreciate in value. *Appreciate* is just another way of saying *grow*. If you bought a stock for $8 per share and now its value is $30 per share, your investment has grown by $22 per share — that's appreciation.

Appreciation (also known as *capital gain*) is probably the number-one reason people invest in stocks. Few investments have the potential to grow your wealth as conveniently as stocks. But they're not the only way. Many investors seek alternative ways to make money, but many of these alternative ways are more aggressive than stocks and carry significantly more risk.

You may have heard about people who made quick fortunes in areas such as commodities (like wheat, pork bellies, or precious metals), options, and other more-sophisticated investment vehicles. Note that you should limit these riskier investments to only a small portion of your portfolio, such as 5 or 10 percent of your investable funds. Experienced investors, however, can go higher.

Income investing

Not all investors want to take on the risk that comes with making a killing. Some people just want to invest in the stock market as a means of providing a steady income. If your purpose for investing in stocks is to create income, you need to choose stocks that pay dividends. Dividends are typically paid quarterly to stockholders on record as of specific dates. How do you know if the dividend you're being paid is higher (or lower) than other vehicles (such as bonds)? The following sections help you figure it out.

Dividends versus interest

Don't confuse dividends with interest. Most people are familiar with interest because that's how you grow your money over the years in the bank. The important difference is that *interest* is paid to creditors, and *dividends* are paid to owners (meaning *shareholders* — and if you own stock, you're a shareholder because shares of stock represent ownership in a publicly traded company).

When you buy stock, you buy a piece of a company. When you put money in a bank (or when you buy bonds), you basically loan your money. You become a creditor, and the bank or bond issuer is the debtor; as such, it must eventually pay your money back to you with interest.

The importance of an income stock's yield

When you invest for income, you have to consider your investment's yield and compare it with the alternatives. The *yield* is an investment's payout expressed as a percentage of the investment amount. Looking at the yield is a way to compare the income you expect to receive from one investment with the expected income from others. Table 2-2 shows some comparative yields.

Investment	Type	Amount	Pay Type	Payout	Yield
Smith Co.	Stock	$50/share	Dividend	$2.50	5.0%
Jones Co.	Stock	$100/share	Dividend	$4.00	4.0%
Acme Bank	Bank CD	$500	Interest	$5.00	1.0%
Acme Bank	Bank CD	$2,500	Interest	$31.25	1.25%
Acme Bank	Bank CD	$5,000	Interest	$75.00	1.50%
Brown Co.	Bond	$5,000	Interest	$300.00	6.0%

Table 2-2: *Comparing the Yields of Various Investments*

Yield equals the payout divided by the investment amount. For the sake of simplicity, the following exercise is based on an annual percentage yield basis (compounding would increase the yield).

Jones Co. and Smith Co. are typical dividend-paying stocks. Looking at Table 2-2 and presuming that both companies are similar in most respects except for their differing dividends, how can you tell whether the $50 stock with a $2.50 annual dividend is better (or worse) than the $100 stock with a $4.00 dividend? The yield tells you.

Even though Jones Co. pays a higher dividend ($4.00), Smith Co. has a higher yield (5 percent). Therefore, if you have to choose between those two stocks as an income investor, you should choose Smith Co. Of course, if you truly want to maximize your income and don't really need your investment to appreciate a lot, you should probably choose Brown Co.'s bond because it offers a yield of 6 percent.

Dividend-paying stocks do have the ability to increase in value. They may not have the same growth potential as growth stocks, but at the very least, they have a greater potential for capital gain than CDs or bonds.

Invest for Your Style

Investing style refers to your approach to stock investing. Do you want to be conservative or aggressive?

Conservative investing

Conservative investing means that you put your money in something proven, tried, and true. You invest your money in safe and secure places, such as banks and government-backed securities.

_____

_____

_____

If you're a conservative stock investor, you want to place your money in companies with the following qualities:

- **Proven performance:** You want companies that have shown increasing sales and earnings year after year. You don't demand anything spectacular — just a strong and steady performance.

- **Large market size:** You want to invest in *large cap* companies (short for *large capitalization*). In other words, they should have a market value exceeding $5–$25 billion. Conservative investors surmise that bigger is safer.

- **Proven market leadership:** Look for companies that are leaders in their industries.

- **Perceived staying power:** You want companies with the financial clout and market position to weather uncertain market and economic conditions. What happens in the economy shouldn't matter.

Aggressive investing

Aggressive investors can plan long term or look over only the intermediate term, but in any case, they want stocks that show the potential to break out of the pack. If you're an aggressive

stock investor, you want to invest your money in companies
that exhibit some of the following qualities:

- **Great potential:** Choose companies that have superior
  goods, services, ideas, or ways of doing business compared to the competition.

- **Capital gains possibility:** Don't even consider dividends. If anything, you dislike dividends. You feel that
  the money dispensed in dividend form is better rein-
  vested in the company. This, in turn, can spur greater
  growth.

- **Innovation:** Find companies that have innovative technologies, ideas, or methods that make them stand apart
  from other companies.

3

Risk and Volatility

Be aware of the different kinds of risk described in this chapter, so you can easily plan around them to keep your money growing. And don't forget volatility, which is about the rapid movement of buying or selling, which, in turn, causes stock prices to rise or fall rapidly. Technically, volatility is considered a "neutral" condition, but it's usually associated with rapid downward movement of stock because that means sudden loss for investors and causes anxiety.

Different Kinds of Risk

Don't let risk frighten you. Just make sure that you understand the different kinds of risk in the following sections before you start navigating the investment world.

Financial risk

The financial risk of stock investing is that you can lose your money if the company whose stock you purchase loses money or goes belly up. This type of risk is the most obvious because companies do go bankrupt.

You can greatly enhance the chances of your financial risk paying off by doing research and choosing stocks carefully. Financial risk is a real concern even when the economy is doing well. Some diligent research, planning, and common sense help you reduce your financial risk.

In terms of financial risk, the bottom line is . . . well . . . the bottom line. A healthy bottom line means that a company is making money. And if a company is making money, then you can make money by investing in its stock. However, if a company isn't making money, you won't make money if you invest in it. Profit is the lifeblood of any company. See Chapter 6 for the scoop on determining whether a company's bottom line is healthy.

Interest rate risk

Interest rate risk may sound like an odd type of risk, but in fact, it's a common consideration for investors. Be aware that interest rates change on a regular basis, causing some challenging moments. Banks set interest rates, and the primary institution to watch closely is the Federal Reserve (the Fed). The Fed raises or lowers its interest rates, actions that, in turn, cause banks to raise or lower their interest rates accordingly. Interest rate changes affect consumers, businesses, and, of course, investors.

Historically, rising interest rates have had an adverse effect on stock prices. I outline several reasons why in the following sections. Because the United States is top-heavy in debt, rising interest rates are an obvious risk that threatens both stocks and fixed-income securities (such as bonds).

A company's financial condition hurt

Rising interest rates have a negative impact on companies that carry a large current debt load or that need to take on more debt because when interest rates rise, the cost of borrowing money rises, too. Ultimately, the company's profitability and ability to grow are reduced. When a company's profits (or earnings) drop, its stock becomes less desirable, and its stock price falls.

_____

_____

_____

A company's customers affected

A company's success comes from selling its products or services. But what happens if increased interest rates negatively impact its customers? The financial health of its customers directly affects the company's ability to grow sales and earnings.

Consider Home Depot (HD) during 2005–2008. The company had soaring sales and earnings during 2005 and into early 2006 as the housing boom hit its high point (record sales, construction, and so on). As the housing bubble popped and the housing and construction industries went into an agonizing decline, the fortunes of Home Depot followed suit because its success is directly tied to home building, repair, and improvement. By late 2006, HD's sales were slipping, and earnings were dropping as the housing industry sank deeper into its depression. This was bad news for stock investors. HD's stock went from more than $44 in 2005 to $21 by October 2008 (a drop of about 52 percent).

The point to keep in mind is that because Home Depot's fortunes are tied to the housing industry, and this industry is very sensitive and vulnerable to rising interest rates, in an indirect — but significant — way, Home Depot is also vulnerable.

In 2015, HD was one of the few retail stocks that went up due to the rebounding real estate market. However, as interest rates ticked up at the end of 2015, the real estate industry started slowing down, which means that HD would be vulnerable in 2016.

Investors' decision-making impacted

When interest rates rise, investors start to rethink their investment strategies, resulting in one of two outcomes:

- Investors may sell any shares in interest-sensitive stocks that they hold. Interest-sensitive industries include electric utilities, real estate, and the financial sector. Although increased interest rates can hurt these sectors, the reverse is also generally true: Falling interest rates boost the same industries. Keep in mind that interest rate changes affect some industries more than others.

- Investors who favor increased current income (versus waiting for the investment to grow in value to sell for a gain later on) are definitely attracted to investment vehicles that offer a higher yield. Higher interest rates can cause investors to switch from stocks to bonds or bank certificates of deposit.

Stock prices indirectly hurt

High or rising interest rates can have a negative impact on any investor's total financial picture. What happens when an investor struggles with burdensome debt, such as a second mortgage, credit card debt, or *margin debt* (debt from borrowing against stock in a brokerage account)? He may sell some stock to pay off some of his high-interest debt. Selling stock to service debt is a common practice that, when taken collectively, can hurt stock prices.

As I write this, the size of the U.S. economy in terms of gross domestic product (GDP) is about $18 trillion (give or take $100 billion), but the debt level is more than $70 trillion (this amount includes personal, corporate, mortgage, college, and government debt). This already enormous amount doesn't include more than $100 trillion of liabilities such as Social Security and Medicare. Additionally, some U.S. financial institutions hold more than 700 trillion dollars' worth of derivatives. These can be very complicated and risky investment vehicles that can backfire. Derivatives have, in fact, sunk some large organizations (such as Enron in 2001, Bear Stearns in 2008, and the trading firm Glencore in 2015), and investors should be aware of them. Just check out the company's financial reports.

Because of the effects of interest rates on stock portfolios, both direct and indirect, successful investors regularly monitor interest rates in both the general economy and in their personal situations. Although stocks have proven to be a superior long-term investment (the longer the term, the better), every investor should maintain a balanced portfolio that includes other investment vehicles. A diversified investor has some money in vehicles that do well when interest rates rise. These vehicles include money market funds, U.S. savings bonds (series I), and other variable-rate investments whose interest rates rise when market rates rise. These types of investments add a measure of safety from interest rate risk to your stock portfolio. (Diversification is discussed in more detail later in this chapter.)

Market risk

People talk about *the market* and how it goes up or down, making it sound like a monolith instead of what it really is —

millions of individuals making daily decisions to buy or sell stock. No matter how modern our society and economic system, you can't escape the laws of supply and demand. When masses of people want to buy a particular stock, it becomes in demand, and its price rises. That price rises higher if the supply is limited. If no one's interested in buying a stock, its price falls. Supply and demand is the nature of market risk. The price of the stock you purchase can rise and fall on the fickle whim of market demand.

Millions of investors buying and selling each minute of every trading day affect the share price of your stock. This fact makes it impossible to judge which way your stock will move tomorrow or next week. This unpredictability and seeming irrationality is why stocks aren't appropriate for short-term financial growth.

Markets are volatile by nature; they go up and down, and investments need time to grow. Market volatility is an increasingly common condition that everyone has to live with (see the later section "The Scoop on Volatility"). Investors should be aware of the fact that stocks in general aren't suitable for short-term (one year or less) goals (see Chapters 1 and 2 for more on short-term goals). Despite the fact that companies you're invested in may be fundamentally sound, all stock prices are subject to the gyrations of the marketplace and need time to trend upward.

Investing requires diligent work and research before putting your money in quality investments with a long-term perspective. Speculating is attempting to make a relatively quick profit by monitoring the short-term price movements of a particular investment. Investors seek to minimize risk, whereas speculators don't mind risk because it can also magnify profits. Speculating and investing have clear differences, but investors frequently become speculators and ultimately put themselves and their wealth at risk.

Consider the married couple nearing retirement who decided to play with their money in an attempt to make their pending retirement more comfortable. They borrowed a sizable sum by tapping into their home equity to invest in the stock market. (Their home, which they had paid off, had enough equity to qualify for this loan.) What did they do with these funds? You guessed it; they invested in the high-flying stocks of the day, which were high-tech and Internet stocks. Within eight months, they lost almost all their money.

Understanding market risk is especially important for people who are tempted to put their nest eggs or emergency funds into volatile investments such as growth stocks. Remember, you can lose everything.

_____

_____

_____

Inflation risk

Inflation is the artificial expansion of the quantity of money so that too much money is used in exchange for goods and services. To consumers, inflation shows up in the form of higher prices for goods and services. Inflation risk is also referred to as *purchasing power risk*. This term just means that your money doesn't buy as much as it used to. For example, a dollar that bought you a sandwich in 1980 barely bought you a candy bar a few years later. For you, the investor, this risk means that the value of your investment (a stock that doesn't appreciate much, for example) may not keep up with inflation.

Say that you have money in a bank savings account currently earning 4 percent. This account has flexibility — if the market interest rate goes up, the rate you earn in your account goes up. Your account is safe from both financial risk and interest rate risk. But what if inflation is running at 5 percent? At that point you're losing money.

Tax risk

Taxes (such as income tax or capital gains tax) don't affect your stock investment directly, but taxes can obviously affect how much of your money you get to keep. Because the entire point of stock investing is to build wealth, you need to understand that taxes take away a portion of the wealth that you're trying to build. Taxes can be risky because if you make the wrong move with your stocks (selling them at the wrong time, for example), you can end up paying higher taxes than you need to. Because tax laws change so frequently, tax risk is part of the risk-versus-return equation, as well.

It pays to gain knowledge about how taxes can impact your wealth-building program before you make your investment decisions. Chapter 10 covers the impact of taxes.

Political and governmental risk

If companies were fish, politics and government policies (such as taxes, laws, and regulations) would be the pond. In the same way that fish die in a toxic or polluted pond, politics and government policies can kill companies. Of course, if you own stock in a company exposed to political and governmental risks, you need to be aware of these risks. For some companies, a single new regulation or law is enough to send them into bankruptcy. For other companies, a new law can help them increase sales and profits.

What if you invest in companies or industries that become political targets? You may want to consider selling them (you can always buy them back later) or consider putting in stop-loss orders on the stock (see Chapter 9). For example, tobacco companies were the targets of political firestorms that battered their stock prices. Whether you agree or disagree with the political machinations of today is not the issue. As an investor, you have to ask yourself, "How do politics affect the market value and the current and future prospects of my chosen investment?"

Keep in mind that political risk doesn't just mean in the United States; it can also mean international political risk. Many companies have operations across many countries, and geopolitical events can have a major impact on those companies exposed to risks ranging from governmental risks (such as in Venezuela at the time of this writing) to war and unrest (as in the Middle East) to recessions and economic downturns in friendly countries (such as in Western Europe).

 If international investing interests you and you see it as a good way to be more diversified (beyond the U.S. stock market), consider exchange-traded funds (ETFs). Find out more about ETFs in Chapter 8.

Personal risk

Frequently, the risk involved with investing in the stock market isn't directly related to the investment; rather, the risk is associated with the investor's circumstances.

Suppose that investor Ralph puts $15,000 into a portfolio of common stocks. Imagine that the market experiences a drop in prices that week, and Ralph's stocks drop to a market value of $14,000. Because stocks are good for the long term, this type of decrease usually isn't an alarming incident. Odds are that this dip is temporary, especially if Ralph carefully chose high-quality companies. Incidentally, if a portfolio of high-quality stocks *does* experience a temporary drop in price, it can be a great opportunity to get more shares at a good price. (Chapter 9 covers orders you can place with your broker to help you do that.)

Over the long term, Ralph will probably see the value of his investment grow substantially. But what if Ralph experiences financial difficulty and needs quick cash during a period when his stocks are declining? He may have to sell his stock to get some money.

This problem occurs frequently for investors who don't have an emergency fund to handle large, sudden expenses. You never know when your company may lay you off or when your basement may flood, leaving you with a huge repair bill.

Car accidents, medical emergencies, and other unforeseen events are part of life's bag of surprises — for anyone.

You probably won't get much comfort from knowing that stock losses are tax-deductible — a loss is a loss (see Chapter 10 for more on taxes). However, you can avoid the kind of loss that results from prematurely having to sell your stocks if you maintain an emergency cash fund. A good place for your emergency cash fund is in either a bank savings account or a money market fund. Then you aren't forced to prematurely liquidate your stock investments to pay emergency bills. (Chapter 1 provides more guidance.)

Emotional risk

Emotions are important risk considerations because investors are human beings. Logic and discipline are critical factors in investment success, but even the best investor can let emotions take over the reins of money management and cause loss. For stock investing, you're likely to be sidetracked by three main emotions: greed, fear, and love. You need to understand your emotions and what kinds of risk they can expose you to.

Greed

In 1998–2000, millions of investors threw caution to the wind and chased highly dubious, risky dot-com stocks. The dollar signs popped up in their eyes when they saw that Easy Street was lined with dot-com stocks that were doubling and tripling in a very short time. Who cares about price/earnings (P/E) ratios when you can just buy stock, make a fortune, and get out with millions? (Of course, *you* care about making money with stocks, so you can flip to Chapter 6 to find out more about P/E ratios.)

Unfortunately, the lure of the easy buck can easily turn healthy attitudes about growing wealth into unhealthy greed that blinds investors and discards common sense. Avoid the temptation to invest for short-term gains in dubious hot stocks instead of doing your homework and buying stocks of solid companies with strong fundamentals and a long-term focus.

Fear

Greed can be a problem, but fear is the other extreme. People who are fearful of loss frequently avoid suitable investments and end up settling for a low rate of return. If you have to succumb to one of these emotions, at least fear exposes you to less loss.

Also, keep in mind that fear is frequently a symptom of lack of knowledge about what's going on. If you see your stocks falling and don't understand why, fear will take over, and you may act irrationally. When stock investors are affected by fear, they tend to sell their stocks and head for the exits and the lifeboats. When an investor sees his stock go down 20 percent, what goes through his head? Experienced, knowledgeable investors realize that no bull market goes straight up. Even the strongest bull goes up in a zigzag fashion. Conversely, even bear markets don't go straight down; they zigzag down. Out of fear, inexperienced investors sell good stocks when they see them go down temporarily (the *correction*), whereas experienced investors see that temporary downward move as a good buying opportunity to add to their positions.

Love

Stocks are dispassionate, inanimate vehicles, but people can look for love in the strangest places. Emotional risk occurs when investors fall in love with a stock and refuse to sell it, even when the stock is plummeting and shows all the symptoms of getting worse. Emotional risk also occurs when investors are drawn to bad investment choices just because they sound good, are popular, or are pushed by family or friends.

_____

_____

_____

Love and attachment are great in relationships with people but can be horrible with investments. To deal with this emotion, investors have to deploy techniques that take the emotion out. For example, you can use brokerage orders (such as trailing stops and limit orders; see Chapter 9), which can automatically trigger buy and sell transactions and leave out some of the agonizing.

The Scoop on Volatility

People may think of volatility as "risk on steroids," but you need to understand what volatility actually is. Technically, it isn't really good or bad (although it's usually associated with bad movements in the marketplace). *Volatility* is the movement of an asset (or the entire market) very quickly down (or up) in price due to large selling (or buying) in a very short period of time.

Volatility tends to be more associated with the negative because of crowd psychology. People are more likely to act quickly (sell) because of fear than because of other motivators (such as greed; see the earlier section "Emotional risk" for more info). More people are apt to run for the exits than they are to run to the entrance, so to speak.

Not all stocks are equal with regard to volatility. Some can be very volatile, whereas others can be quite stable. A good way to determine a stock's volatility is to look at the beta of the stock. *Beta* is a statistical measure that attempts to give the investor a clue as to how volatile a stock may be. It's determined by comparing the potential volatility of a particular stock to the market in general. The market (as represented by, say, the Standard & Poor's 500) is assigned a beta of 1. Any stock with a beta greater than 1 is considered more volatile than the general stock market, whereas any stock with a beta of less than 1 is considered less volatile. If a stock has a beta of 1.5, for example, it's considered 50 percent more volatile than the general market. Meanwhile, a stock with a beta of 0.85 is considered 15 percent less volatile than the general stock market. In other words, this stock would decline 8.5 percent if the market were to decline 10 percent.

Consider stocks that have a beta of less than 1. You can find the beta in the stock report pages that are usually provided by major financial websites such as Yahoo! Finance (`finance.yahoo.com`) and MarketWatch (`www.marketwatch.com`).

Minimize Your Risk

Minimizing your risk in stock investing is easier than you think. Although building wealth through the stock market doesn't take place without some amount of risk, you can practice the following tips to maximize your profits and still keep your money secure.

Gain knowledge

Lack of knowledge constitutes the greatest risk for new investors, so diminishing that risk starts with gaining knowledge. The more familiar you are with the stock market — how it works, factors that affect stock value, and so on — the better you can navigate around its pitfalls and maximize your profits. The same knowledge that enables you to grow your wealth also enables you to minimize your risk. Before you put your money anywhere, you want to know as much as you can. Check out Chapter 4 for a rundown of the kinds of information you want to know before you buy stocks, as well as the resources that can give you the information you need to invest successfully.

Stay out until you get a little practice

If you don't understand stocks, don't invest. I think that some measure of stock investing is a good idea for most people, but that doesn't mean you should be 100 percent invested 100 percent of the time. If you don't understand a particular stock (or don't understand stocks, period), stay away until you do. Instead, give yourself an imaginary sum of money, such as $100,000, give yourself reasons to invest, and just make believe (a practice called *simulated stock investing*). Pick a few stocks that you think will increase in value, track them for a while, and see how they perform. Begin to understand how the price of a stock goes up and down, and watch what happens to the stocks you choose when various events take place. As you find out more about stock investing, you get better at picking individual stocks, without risking — or losing — any money during your learning period.

A good place to do your imaginary investing is at a website such as Investopedia's simulator (www.investopedia.com/simulator).

_____

_____

_____

Put your financial house in order

You want to make sure that you are, first and foremost, financially secure before you take the plunge into the stock market. If you're not sure about your financial security, look over your situation with a financial planner.

Before you buy your first stock, here are a few things you can do to get your finances in order:

- **Have a cushion of money.** Set aside three to six months' worth of your gross living expenses somewhere safe, such as in a bank account or treasury money market fund, in case you suddenly need cash for an emergency (see Chapter 1 for details).

- **Reduce your debt.** Overindulging in debt has been the worst personal economic problem for many Americans in recent years.

- **Make sure that your job is as secure as you can make it.** Are you keeping your skills up to date? Is the company you work for strong and growing? Is the industry that you work in strong and growing?

- **Make sure that you have adequate insurance.** You need enough insurance to cover your needs and those of your family in case of illness, death, disability, and so on.

Diversify your investments

Diversification is a strategy for reducing risk by spreading your money across different investments. It's a fancy way of saying, "Don't put all your eggs in one basket." But how do you go about divvying up your money and distributing it among different investments?

The easiest way to understand proper diversification may be to look at what you *shouldn't* do:

- **Don't put all your money in one stock.** Sure, if you choose wisely and select a hot stock, you may make a bundle, but the odds are tremendously against you. Unless you're a real expert on a particular company, it's a good idea to have small portions of your money in several different stocks. As a general rule, the money you tie up in a single stock should be money you can do without.

- **Don't put all your money in one industry.** I know people who own several stocks, but the stocks are all in the same industry. Again, if you're an expert in that particular industry, it can work out. But just understand that you're not properly diversified. If a problem hits an entire industry, you may get hurt.

- **Don't put all your money in one type of investment.** Stocks may be a great investment, but you need to have money elsewhere. Bonds, bank accounts, treasury securities, real estate, and precious metals are perennial alternatives to complement your stock portfolio. Some of these alternatives can be found in mutual funds or exchange-traded funds (ETFs). An *exchange-traded fund* is a fund with a fixed portfolio of stocks or other securities that tracks a particular index but is traded like a stock. (See Chapter 8 for more information.)

Okay, what *should* you do? Until you become more knowledgeable, follow this advice:

- **Keep only 5 to 10 percent (or less) of your investment money in a single stock.** Because you want adequate diversification, you don't want overexposure to a single stock. Aggressive investors can certainly go for 10 percent or even higher, but conservative investors are better off at 5 percent or less.

- **Invest in four or five (and no more than ten) different stocks that are in different industries.** Choose industries that offer products and services that have shown strong, growing demand. Think about the industries that people need no matter what happens in the general economy, such as food, energy, and other consumer necessities. See Chapter 7 for more information about analyzing sectors and industries.

Weigh Risk against Return

How much risk is appropriate for you, and how do you handle it? Before you try to figure out what risks accompany your investment choices, analyze yourself. Here are some points to keep in mind:

- **Your financial goal:** In five minutes with a calculator, you can see how much money you're going to need to become financially independent (presuming financial independence is your goal). Say that you need $500,000 in ten years for a worry-free retirement and that your financial assets (such as stocks, bonds, and so on) are currently worth $400,000. In this scenario, your assets need to grow by only 2.25 percent to hit your target. Getting investments that grow by 2.25 percent safely is easy to do because that's a relatively low rate of return.

The important point is that you don't have to knock yourself out trying to double your money with risky, high-flying investments; some run-of-the-mill bank investments will do just fine. All too often, investors take on more risk than is necessary. Figure out what your financial goal is so that you know what kind of return you realistically need. Flip to Chapters 1 and 2 for details on determining your financial goals.

- **Your investor profile:** If you're just beginning your working years, you can tolerate greater risk than someone facing retirement. Even if you lose big, you still have time to recoup your money.

  However, if you're within five years of retirement, risky or aggressive investments can do much more harm than good. If you lose money, you don't have as much time to recoup your investment, and odds are that you'll need the investment money (and its income-generating capacity) to cover your living expenses after you're no longer employed.

- **Asset allocation:** I never tell retirees to put a large portion of their retirement money into a high-tech stock or other volatile investment. But if they still want to speculate, I don't see a problem as long as they limit such investments to 5 percent of their total assets. The bulk of their money should be safe and sound in secure investments.

Asset allocation beckons back to diversification, discussed earlier in this chapter. For people in their 20s and 30s, having 75 percent of their money in a diversified portfolio of growth stocks (such as mid cap and small cap stocks) is acceptable. For people in their 60s and 70s, it's not acceptable. They may, instead, consider investing no more than 20 percent of their money in stocks (mid caps and large caps are preferable). Check with your financial advisor to find the right mix for your particular situation.

4

Gathering Information

For the best approach to stock investing, build your knowledge and find quality information first so you can make your fortunes more assuredly. Before you buy, you need to know that the company you're investing in is

- Financially sound and growing
- Offering products and/or services that are in demand by consumers
- In a strong and growing industry (and general economy)

Where do you start, and what kind of information do you want to acquire? Keep reading.

Look to Stock Exchanges for Answers

Before you invest in stocks, you need to be completely familiar with the basics of stock investing. At its most fundamental, stock investing is about using your money to buy a piece of a company that will give you value in the form of appreciation or income (or both). Fortunately, many resources are available to help you find out about stock investing. Some of my favorite places are the stock exchanges themselves.

Stock exchanges are organized marketplaces for the buying and selling of stocks (and other securities). The New York Stock Exchange (NYSE; also referred to as the *Big Board*), the premier stock exchange, provides a framework for stock buyers and sellers to make their transactions. The NYSE makes money not only from a cut of every transaction but also from fees (such as listing fees) charged to companies and brokers that are members of its exchanges. In 2007, the NYSE merged with Euronext, a major European exchange, but no material differences exist for stock investors. In 2009, the American Stock Exchange (Amex) was taken over by (and completely merged into) the NYSE. The new name is NYSE Amex.

The main exchanges for most stock investors are the NYSE and Nasdaq. Technically, Nasdaq isn't an exchange, but it's a formal market that effectively acts as an exchange. Because the NYSE and Nasdaq benefit from increased popularity of stock investing and continued demand for stocks, they offer a wealth of free (or low-cost) resources and information for stock investors.

 What each exchange/market offers keeps changing and is often updated, so explore them periodically at their respective websites:

- New York Stock Exchange: www.nyse.com
- Nasdaq: www.nasdaq.com

The Basics of Accounting and Economics

Stocks represent ownership in companies. Before you buy individual stocks, you want to understand the companies whose stock you're considering and find out about their operations. It may sound like a daunting task, but you'll digest the point more easily when you realize that companies work very similarly to the way you work. They make decisions on a daily basis just as you do. Low earnings and high debt are examples of financial difficulties that can affect both people and companies.

You can better understand companies' finances by taking the time to pick up some information in two basic disciplines: accounting and economics. These two disciplines play a significant role in understanding the performance of a firm's stock.

Accounting principles

Accounting is the language of business, and believe it or not, you're already familiar with the most important accounting concepts. Just look at the following three essential principles:

- **Assets minus liabilities equals net worth.** In other words, take what you own (your *assets*), subtract what you owe (your *liabilities*), and the rest is yours (your *net worth*). Your own personal finances work the same way as Microsoft's (except yours have fewer zeros at the end). See Chapter 1 to figure out how to calculate your own net worth.

A company's *balance sheet* shows you its net worth at a specific point in time (such as December 31). The net worth of a company is the bottom line of its asset and liability picture, and it tells you whether the company is *solvent* (has the ability to pay its debts without going out of business). The net worth of a successful company grows regularly. To see whether your company is successful, compare its net worth with the net worth from the same point a year earlier. A firm that has a $4 million net worth on December 31, 2016, and a $5 million net worth on December 31, 2017, is doing well; its net worth has gone up 25 percent ($1 million) in one year.

- **Income minus expenses equals net income.** In other words, take what you make (your *income*), subtract what you spend (your *expenses*), and the remainder is your *net income* (or *net profit* or *net earnings* — your gain).

A company's profitability is the whole point of investing in its stock. As it profits, the business becomes more valuable, and in turn, its stock price becomes more valuable. To discover a firm's net income, look at its income statement. Try to determine whether the company uses its gains wisely, either by reinvesting them for continued growth or by paying down debt.

- **Do a comparative financial analysis.** That's a mouthful, but it's just a fancy way of saying how a company is doing now compared with something else (like a prior period or a similar company).

  If you know that the company you're looking at had a net income of $50,000 for the year, you may ask, "Is that good or bad?" Obviously, making a net profit is good, but you also need to know whether it's good compared to something else. If the company had a net profit of $40,000 the year before, you know that the company's profitability is improving. But if a similar company had a net profit of $100,000 the year before and in the current year is making $50,000, then you may want to either avoid the company making the lesser profit or see what (if anything) went wrong with the company making less.

For more information on how to use a company's financial statements to pick good stocks, see Chapter 6.

How economics affects stocks

A working knowledge of basic economics is crucial to your success and proficiency as a stock investor. The stock market and the economy are joined at the hip. The good (or bad) things that happen to one have a direct effect on the other.

Understanding basic economics helps me (and will help you) filter the financial news to separate relevant information from the irrelevant in order to make better investment decisions. Be aware of these important concepts:

- **Supply and demand:** *Supply and demand* can be simply stated as the relationship between what's available (the supply) and what people want and are willing to pay for (the demand). This equation is the main engine of economic activity and is extremely important for your stock investing analysis and decision-making process.

- **Cause and effect:** If you pick up a prominent news report and read, "Companies in the table industry are expecting plummeting sales," do you rush out and invest in companies that sell chairs or manufacture tablecloths? Considering cause and effect is an exercise in logical thinking, and logic is a major component of sound economic thought.

  When you read business news, play it out in your mind. What good (or bad) can logically be expected given a certain event or situation? If you're looking for an effect

("I want a stock price that keeps increasing"), you also want to understand the cause.

Here are some typical events that can cause a stock's price to rise: positive news about a company, positive news about a company's industry, positive news about a company's customers, and negative news about a company's competitors.

- **Economic effects from government actions:** Nothing has a greater effect on investing and economics than government. Government actions usually manifest themselves as taxes, laws, or regulations. They also can take on a more ominous appearance, such as war or the threat of war. Government can cause a company to go bankrupt, disrupt an entire industry, or cause a depression. Government controls the money supply, credit, and all public securities markets.

 Important lessons for investors today include the following:

- Stocks are not a replacement for savings accounts. Always have some money in the bank.
- Stocks should never occupy 100 percent of your investment funds.

- When anyone (including an expert) tells you that the economy will keep growing indefinitely, be skeptical and read diverse sources of information.
- If stocks do well in your portfolio, consider protecting your stocks with stop-loss orders. (See Chapter 9 for more on these strategies.)
- Keep debt and expenses to a minimum.
- If the economy is booming, a decline is sure to follow as the ebb and flow of the economy's business cycle continues.

Read Financial News

Reading the financial news can help you decide where or where not to invest. Many newspapers, magazines, and websites offer great coverage of the financial world. The following sections describe the types of information you need to get from the financial news.

Be sure to check out the following resources:

- The most obvious publications of interest to stock investors are *The Wall Street Journal* (www.wsj.com) and *Investor's Business Daily* (www.investors.com).

- Some of the more obvious websites are MarketWatch (www.marketwatch.com), Yahoo! Finance (http://finance.yahoo.com), Bloomberg (www.bloomberg.com), and Investing.com (www.investing.com).

- Don't forget the websites that I list in the earlier section "Look to Stock Exchanges for Answers."

Figure out what a company's up to

Before you invest, you need to know what's going on with a company. When you read about a company, either from the firm's literature or from media sources, be sure to get answers to some pertinent questions:

- **Is the company making more net income than it did last year?** You want to invest in a company that's growing.

_____

_____

_____

- **Are the company's sales greater than they were the year before?** Keep in mind that you won't make money if the company isn't making money.

- **Is the company issuing press releases on new products, services, inventions, or business deals?** All these achievements indicate a strong, vital company.

Discover what's new with an industry

As you consider investing in a stock, make a point of knowing what's going on in that company's industry. If the industry is doing well, your stock is likely to do well, too. But then again, the reverse is also true.

Yes, I've seen investors pick successful stocks in a failing industry, but those cases are exceptional. By and large, it's easier to succeed with a stock when the entire industry is doing well. As you're watching the news, reading the financial pages, or viewing financial websites, check out the industry to ensure that it's strong and dynamic. See Chapter 7 for information on analyzing sectors and megatrends.

Know the news in the economy

No matter how well or how poorly the overall economy is performing, you want to stay informed about its general progress. It's easier for the value of stock to keep going up when the economy is stable or growing. The reverse is also true: If the economy is contracting or declining, the stock has a tougher time keeping its value. Some basic items to keep tabs on include

- **Gross domestic product (GDP):** The GDP is roughly the total value of output for a particular nation, measured in the dollar amount of goods and services. It's reported quarterly, and a rising GDP bodes well for your stock. When the GDP is rising 3 percent or more on an annual basis, that's solid growth. If it rises but is less than 3 percent, that's generally considered less than stellar (or mediocre). A GDP under zero (a negative number) means that the economy is shrinking (heading into recession).

- **The index of leading economic indicators (LEI):** The LEI is a snapshot of a set of economic statistics covering activity that precedes what's happening in the economy. Each statistic helps you understand the economy in much the same way that barometers help you understand what's happening with the weather. Economists don't just look at an individual statistic; they look at a set of statistics to get a more complete picture of what's happening with the economy.

See what officials are doing

Being informed about what public officials are doing is vital to your success as a stock investor. Because federal, state, and local governments pass thousands of laws, rules, and regulations every year, monitoring the political landscape is critical. Always ask yourself, "How does a new law, tax, or regulation affect my stock investment?"

You can find laws being proposed or enacted by the federal government through the Thomas legislative search engine (http://thomas.loc.gov/home/thomas.php), which is run by the Library of Congress (www.loc.gov). Also, some great organizations inform the public about tax laws and their impact, such as the National Taxpayers Union (www.ntu.org).

Stock Tables

The stock tables in major business publications such as *The Wall Street Journal* and *Investor's Business Daily* are loaded with information that can help you become a savvy investor — *if* you know how to interpret them. You need the information in the stock tables for more than selecting promising investment opportunities. You also need to consult the tables after you invest to monitor how your stocks are doing.

Table 4-1 shows a sample stock table. Each item gives you some clues about the current state of affairs for that particular company. The sections that follow describe each column to help you understand what you're looking at.

52-Wk High	52-Wk Low	Name (Symbol)	Div	Vol	Yld	P/E	Day Last	Net Chg
21.50	8.00	SkyHighCorp (SHC)		3,143		76	21.25	+.25
47.00	31.75	LowDownInc (LDI)	2.35	2,735	5.9	18	41.00	−.50
25.00	21.00	ValueNowInc (VNI)	1.00	1,894	4.5	12	22.00	+.10
83.00	33.00	DoinBadlyCorp (DBC)		7,601			33.50	−.75

Table 4-1: *A Sample Stock Table*

Every newspaper's financial tables are a little different, but they give you basically the same information. Updated daily, these tables aren't the place to start your search for a good stock; they're usually where your search ends. The stock tables are the place to look when you own a stock or know what you want to buy and you're just checking to see the most recent price.

52-week high

The column in Table 4-1 labeled "52-Wk High" gives you the highest price that particular stock has reached in the most recent 52-week period. Knowing this price lets you gauge where the stock is now versus where it has been recently. SkyHighCorp's (SHC) stock has been as high as $21.50, whereas its last (most recent) price is $21.25, the number listed in the "Day Last" column. SkyHighCorp's stock is trading very high right now because it's hovering right near its overall 52-week high figure.

Now, take a look at DoinBadlyCorp's (DBC) stock price. It seems to have tumbled big-time. Its stock price has had a high in the past 52 weeks of $83, but it's currently trading at $33.50. Something just doesn't seem right here. During the past 52 weeks, DBC's stock price has fallen dramatically. If you're thinking about investing in DBC, find out why the stock price

has fallen. If the company is strong, it may be a good opportunity to buy stock at a lower price. If the company is having
tough times, avoid it. In any case, research the firm and find
out why its stock has declined. (Chapter 6 provides the basics
of researching companies.)

52-week low

The column labeled "52-Wk Low" gives you the lowest price
that particular stock reached in the most recent 52-week period.
Again, this information is crucial to your ability to analyze
stock over a period of time. Look at DBC in Table 4-1, and you
can see that its current trading price of $33.50 in the "Day Last"
column is close to its 52-week low of $33.

Keep in mind that the high and low prices just give you a
range of how far a particular stock's price has moved within
the past 52 weeks. They can alert you that a stock has problems
or tell you that a stock's price has fallen enough to make it a
bargain. Simply reading the "52-Wk High" and "52-Wk Low"
columns isn't enough to determine which of those two scenarios is happening. They basically tell you to get more information before you commit your money.

Name and symbol

The "Name (Symbol)" column is the simplest in Table 4-1. It tells you the company name (usually abbreviated) and the stock symbol assigned to the company.

When you have your eye on a stock for potential purchase, get familiar with its symbol. Knowing the symbol makes it easier for you to find your stock in the financial tables, which list stocks in alphabetical order by the company's name (or symbol depending on the source). Stock symbols are the language of stock investing, and you need to use them in all stock communications, from getting a stock quote at your broker's office to buying stock over the Internet.

Dividend

Dividends (shown under the "Div" column in Table 4-1) are basically payments to owners (stockholders). If a company pays a dividend, it's shown in the dividend column. The amount you see is the annual dividend quoted for one share of that stock. If you look at LowDownInc (LDI) in Table 4-1, you can see that you get $2.35 as an annual dividend for each share of stock that you own. Companies usually pay the dividend in quarterly amounts. If I own 100 shares of LDI, the company pays me a quarterly dividend of $58.75 ($235 total per year). A healthy company strives to maintain or upgrade the dividend for stockholders from year to year. (Additional dividend details are discussed later in this chapter.)

Volume

Normally, when you hear the word "volume" on the news, it refers to how much stock is bought and sold for the entire market: "Well, stocks were very active today. Trading volume at the New York Stock Exchange hit 2 billion shares." Volume is certainly important to watch because the stocks that you're investing in are somewhere in that activity. For the "Vol" column in Table 4-1, though, the volume refers to the individual stock.

Volume tells you how many shares of that particular stock were traded that day. If only 100 shares are traded in a day, then the trading volume is 100. SHC had 3,143 shares change hands on the trading day represented in Table 4-1. Is that good or bad? Neither, really. Usually the business news media mention volume for a particular stock only when it's unusually large. If a stock normally has volume in the 5,000 to 10,000 range and all of a sudden has a trading volume of 87,000, then it's time to sit up and take notice.

_____

_____

_____

Keep in mind that a low trading volume for one stock may be a high trading volume for another stock. You can't necessarily compare one stock's volume against that of any other company. The large cap stocks like IBM or Microsoft typically have trading volumes in the millions of shares almost every day, whereas less active, smaller stocks may have average trading volumes in far, far smaller numbers.

The main point to remember is that trading volume that is far in excess of a stock's normal range is a sign that something is going on with that stock. It may be negative or positive, but something newsworthy is happening with that company. If the news is positive, the increased volume is a result of more people buying the stock. If the news is negative, the increased volume is probably a result of more people selling the stock.

Yield

In general, yield is a return on the money you invest. However, in the stock tables, *yield* ("Yld" in Table 4-1) is a reference to what percentage that particular dividend is of the stock price. It's calculated by dividing the annual dividend by the current stock price. In Table 4-1, you can see that the yield of ValueNowInc (VNI) is 4.5 percent (a dividend of $1 divided by the company's stock price of $22). Notice that many companies report no yield; because they have no dividends, their yield is zero.

Keep in mind that the yield reported on the financial sites changes daily as the stock price changes. Yield is always reported as if you're buying the stock that day. If you buy VNI on the day represented in Table 4-1, your yield is 4.5 percent. But what if VNI's stock price rises to $30 the following day? Investors who buy stock at $30 per share obtain a yield of just 3.3 percent (the dividend of $1 divided by the new stock price, $30). Of course, because you bought the stock at $22, you essentially locked in the prior yield of 4.5 percent.

P/E

The *P/E ratio* is the ratio between the price of a stock and the company's earnings. P/E ratios are widely followed and are important barometers of value in the world of stock investing. The P/E ratio (also called the *earnings multiple* or just *multiple*) is frequently used to determine whether a stock is expensive (a good value). Value investors find P/E ratios to be essential to analyzing a stock as a potential investment. As a general rule, the P/E should be 10 to 20 for large cap or income stocks. For growth stocks, a P/E no greater than 30 to 40 is preferable. (See Chapter 6 for full details on P/E ratios.)

_____

_____

_____

In the P/E ratios reported in stock tables, *price* refers to the cost of a single share of stock. *Earnings* refers to the company's reported earnings per share as of the most recent four quarters. The P/E ratio is the price divided by the earnings. In Table 4-1, VNI has a reported P/E of 12, which is considered a low P/E. Notice how SHC has a relatively high P/E (76). This stock is considered too pricey because you're paying a price equivalent to 76 times earnings. Also notice that DBC has no available P/E ratio. Usually this lack of a P/E ratio indicates that the company reported a loss in the most recent four quarters.

Day last

The "Day Last" column tells you how trading ended for a particular stock on the day represented by the table. In Table 4-1, LDI ended the most recent day of trading at $41. Some newspapers report the high and low for that day in addition to the stock's ending price for the day.

Net change

The information in the "Net Chg" column answers the question, "How did the stock price end today compared with its price at the end of the prior trading day?" Table 4-1 shows that SHC stock ended the trading day up 25 cents (at $21.25). This column tells you that SHC ended the prior day at $21.

Use News about Dividends

Reading and understanding the news about dividends is essential if you're an *income investor* (someone who invests in stocks as a means of generating regular income). The following sections explain some basics you should know about dividends.

Look at important dates

To understand how buying stocks that pay dividends can benefit you as an investor, you need to know how companies report and pay dividends. Some important dates in the life of a dividend are as follows:

- **Date of declaration:** This is the date when a company reports a quarterly dividend and the subsequent payment dates. On January 15, for example, a company may report that it "is pleased to announce a quarterly dividend of 50 cents per share to shareholders of record as of February 10." The date of declaration is just the announcement date. Whether you buy the stock before, on, or after the date of declaration doesn't matter in regard to receiving the stock's quarterly dividend. The date that matters is the date of record (see that bullet later in this list).

- **Date of execution:** This is the day you actually initiate the stock transaction (buying or selling). If you call a broker (or contact her online) today to buy a particular stock, then today is the date of execution, or the date on which you execute the trade. You don't own the stock on the date of execution; it's just the day you put in the order. For an example, skip to the following section.

- **Closing date (settlement date):** This is the date on which the trade is finalized, which usually happens three business days after the date of execution. The closing date for stock is similar in concept to a real estate closing. On the closing date, you're officially the proud new owner (or happy seller) of the stock.

- **Ex-dividend date:** *Ex-dividend* means *without dividend*. Because it takes two days to process a stock purchase before you become an official owner of the stock, you have to qualify (that is, you have to own or buy the stock) *before* the two-day period. That two-day period is referred to as the "ex-dividend period." When you buy stock during this short time frame, you aren't on the books of record, because the closing (or settlement) date falls after the date of record. See the next section to see the effect that the ex-dividend date can have on an investor.

- **Date of record:** This is used to identify which stock-holders qualify to receive the declared dividend. Because stock is bought and sold every day, how does the company know which investors to pay? The company establishes a cut-off date by declaring a date of record. All investors who are official stockholders as of the declared date of record receive the dividend on the payment date, even if they plan to sell the stock any time between the date of declaration and the date of record.

- **Payment date:** The date on which a company issues and mails its dividend checks to shareholders.

For typical dividends, the events in Table 4-2 happen four times per year.

Event	Sample Date	Comments
Date of declaration	January 15	The date that the company declares the quarterly dividend
Ex-dividend date	February 8	Starts the two-day period during which, if you buy the stock, you don't qualify for the dividend
Date of record	February 10	The date by which you must be on the books of record to qualify for the dividend
Payment date	February 27	The date that payment is made (a dividend check is issued and mailed to stockholders who were on the books of record as of February 10)

Table 4-2: *The Life of the Quarterly Dividend*

Why certain dates matter

Two business days pass between the date of execution and the closing date. Two business days also pass between the ex-dividend date and the date of record. This information is important to know if you want to qualify to receive an upcoming dividend. Timing is important, and if you understand these dates, you know when to purchase stock and whether you qualify for a dividend.

Say that you want to buy ValueNowInc (VNI) in time to qualify for the quarterly dividend of 25 cents per share.

Assume that the date of record (the date by which you have to be an official owner of the stock) is February 10. You have to execute the trade (buy the stock) no later than February 8 to be assured of the dividend. If you execute the trade right on February 8, the closing date occurs two days later, on February 10 — just in time for the date of record.

But what if you execute the trade on February 9, a day later? Well, the trade's closing date is February 11, which occurs *after* the date of record. Because you aren't on the books as an official stockholder on the date of record, you aren't getting that quarterly dividend. In this example, the February 8–10 period is called the *ex-dividend period*.

Fortunately, for those people who buy the stock during this brief ex-dividend period, the stock actually trades at a slightly lower price to reflect the amount of the dividend. If you can't get the dividend, you may as well save on the stock purchase.

5

Working with Brokers

When you want to buy stock, your task is to do all the research you can to select the company you want to invest in. Still, you need a broker to actually buy the stock, whether you buy over the phone or online. This chapter introduces you to the intricacies of the investor/broker relationship.

The Broker's Role

The broker's primary role is to serve as the vehicle through which you either buy or sell stock. When I talk about brokers, I'm referring to companies that can buy stock on your behalf. Brokers can also be individuals who work for such firms.

The distinction between institutional stockbrokers and personal stockbrokers is important:

- **Institutional stockbrokers** make money from institutions and companies through investment banking and securities placement fees (such as initial public offerings and secondary offerings), advisory services, and other broker services.

- **Personal stockbrokers** generally offer the same services to individuals and small businesses.

Personal stockbrokers make their money from individual investors through various fees, including the following:

- **Brokerage commissions:** This fee is for buying and/or selling stocks and other securities.

- **Margin interest charges:** This interest is charged to investors for borrowing against their brokerage account for investment purposes. (Margin accounts are discussed in more detail later in this chapter.)

- **Service charges:** These charges are for performing administrative tasks and other functions. Brokers charge fees to investors for Individual Retirement Accounts (IRAs) and for mailing stocks in certificate form.

_____

_____

_____

Any broker (some brokers are now called *financial advisors*) you deal with should be registered with the Financial Industry Regulatory Authority (FINRA) and the Securities and Exchange Commission (SEC). In addition, to protect your money after you deposit it into a brokerage account, that broker should be a member of the Securities Investor Protection Corporation (SIPC). SIPC doesn't protect you from market losses; it protects your money in case the brokerage firm goes out of business or if your losses are due to brokerage fraud. To find out whether the broker is registered with these organizations, contact FINRA (www.finra.org), the SEC (www.sec.gov), or SIPC (www.sipc.org).

Types of Brokers

Stockbrokers fall into two basic categories, discussed in the following sections: full-service and discount. The type you choose really depends on what type of investor you are. Here are the differences in a nutshell:

- **Full-service brokers** are suitable for investors who need some guidance and personal attention.
- **Discount brokers** are better for those investors who are sufficiently confident and knowledgeable about stock investing to manage with minimal help (usually through the broker's website).

Before you deal with any broker (either full-service or discount), get a free report on the broker from FINRA by calling 800-289-9999 or through its website at www. finra.org. Through its service called BrokerCheck, you can get a report on either a brokerage firm or an individual broker. FINRA can tell you in its report whether any complaints or penalties have been filed against a brokerage firm or an individual rep.

Full-service brokers

Full-service brokers are just what the name indicates. They try to provide as many services as possible for investors who open accounts with them. When you open an account at a brokerage firm, a representative is assigned to your account. This representative is usually called an *account executive*, a *registered rep*, or a *financial advisor* by the brokerage firm. This person usually has a securities license (meaning that she's registered with FINRA and the SEC) and is knowledgeable about stocks in particular and investing in general.

Examples of full-service brokers are Merrill Lynch and Morgan Stanley. Of course, all brokers now have full-featured websites to give you further information about their services. Get as informed as possible before you open your account.

What they can do for you

Your account executive is responsible for assisting you, answering questions about your account and the securities in your portfolio, and transacting your buy and sell orders. Here are some things that full-service brokers can do for you:

- **Offer guidance and advice:** The greatest distinction between full-service brokers and discount brokers is the personal attention you receive from your account rep. You get to be on a first-name basis with a full-service broker, and you disclose much information about your finances and financial goals. The rep is there to make recommendations about stocks and funds that are hopefully suitable for you.

- **Provide access to research:** Full-service brokers can give you access to their investment research department, which can give you in-depth information and analysis on a particular company. This information can be very valuable, but be aware of the pitfalls. (See the later section "Judge Brokers' Advice.")

- **Help you achieve your investment objectives:** A good rep gets to know you and your investment goals and *then* offers advice and answers your questions about how specific investments and strategies can help you accomplish your wealth-building goals.

- **Make investment decisions on your behalf:** Many investors don't want to be bothered when it comes to investment decisions. Full-service brokers can actually make decisions for your account with your authorization (this is also referred to as a *discretionary* account, although many brokers have scaled back the use of discretion for ordinary brokerage accounts). This service is fine, but be sure to require brokers to explain their choices to you.

What to watch out for

Although full-service brokers, with their seemingly limitless assistance, can make life easy for an investor, you need to remember some important points to avoid problems:

- Brokers and account reps are salespeople. No matter how well they treat you, they're still compensated based on their ability to produce revenue for the brokerage firm. They generate commissions and fees from you on behalf of the company.

- Whenever your rep makes a suggestion or recommendation, be sure to ask why and request a complete answer that includes the reasoning behind the recommendation. A good advisor is able to clearly explain the reasoning behind every suggestion. If you don't fully understand and agree with the advice, don't take it.

- Working with a full-service broker costs more than working with a discount broker. Discount brokers are paid for simply buying or selling stocks for you. Full-service brokers do that and much more, like provide advice and guidance. Because of that, full-service brokers are more expensive (through higher brokerage commissions and advisory fees). Also, most full-service brokers expect you to invest at least $5,000 to $10,000 just to open an account, although many require higher minimums.

- Handing over decision-making authority to your rep can be a possible negative because letting others make financial decisions for you is always dicey — especially when they're using *your* money. If they make poor investment choices that lose you money, you may not have any recourse because you authorized them to act on your behalf.

Discount brokers

Perhaps you don't need any hand-holding from a broker. You know what you want, and you can make your own investment decisions. All you need is a convenient way to transact your buy/sell orders. In that case, go with a discount broker. They don't offer advice or premium services — just the basics required to perform your stock transactions.

Discount brokers, as the name implies, are cheaper to engage than full-service brokers. Because you're advising yourself (or getting advice and information from third parties such as newsletters, hotlines, or independent advisors), you can save on costs that you'd incur if you used a full-service broker.

If you choose to work with a discount broker, you must know as much as possible about your personal goals and needs. You have a greater responsibility for conducting adequate research to make good stock selections, and you must be prepared to accept the outcome, whatever that may be.

For a while, the regular investor had two types of discount brokers to choose from: conventional discount brokers and Internet discount brokers. Through industry consolidation, most of the conventional discount brokers today have full-featured websites, while Internet discount brokers have adapted by adding more telephone and face-to-face services.

Charles Schwab and TD Ameritrade are conventional discount brokers that have adapted well to the Internet era. Internet brokers such as E*TRADE (us.etrade.com), TradeKing (www.tradeking.com), Scottrade (www.scottrade.com), and thinkorswim (www.thinkorswim.com) have added conventional services.

What they can do for you

Discount brokers offer some significant advantages over full-service brokers, such as

_____

_____

_____

- **Lower cost:** This lower cost is usually the result of lower commissions.

- **Unbiased service:** Because they don't offer advice, discount brokers have no vested interest in trying to sell you any particular stock.

- **Access to information:** Established discount brokers offer extensive educational materials.

What to watch out for

Of course, doing business with discount brokers also has its downsides, including the following:

- **No guidance:** Because you've chosen a discount broker, you *know* not to expect guidance, but the broker should make this fact clear to you anyway. If you're a knowledgeable investor, the lack of advice is considered a positive thing — no interference.

- **Hidden fees:** Discount brokers may shout about their lower commissions, but commissions aren't their only way of making money. Many discount brokers charge extra for services that you may think are included, such as issuing a stock certificate or mailing a statement. Ask whether they assess fees for maintaining IRAs or for transferring stocks and other securities (like bonds) in or out of your account, and find out what interest rates they charge for borrowing through brokerage accounts.

- **Minimal customer service:** If you deal with an Internet broker, find out about its customer service capability. If you can't transact business on its website, find out where you can call for assistance.

Choose a Broker

Before you choose a broker, you need to analyze your personal investing style (see Chapter 2), and then you can proceed to finding the kind of broker that fits your needs. Keep the following points in mind:

- Match your investment style with a brokerage firm that charges the least amount of money for the services you're likely to use most frequently.

- Compare all the costs of buying, selling, and holding stocks and other securities through a broker. Don't compare only commissions; compare other costs, too, like margin interest and other service charges (see the earlier section "The Broker's Role" for more info).

_____

_____

_____

- Use broker comparison services available in financial publications such as *Kiplinger's Personal Finance* and *Barron's* (and, of course, their websites) as well as online sources.

Brokers are listed in the Yellow Pages (or on directory sites like www.superpages.com), in many investment publications, and on many financial websites.

Types of Brokerage Accounts

Most brokerage firms offer investors several types of accounts, each serving a different purpose. Three of the most common types are presented in the following sections. The basic difference boils down to how particular brokers view your creditworthiness when it comes to buying and selling securities.

To open an account, you have to fill out an application and submit a check or money order for at least the minimum amount required to establish an account.

Cash accounts

A *cash account* (also referred to as a *Type 1 account*) means just what you'd think. You must deposit a sum of money along with the new account application to begin trading. The amount of your initial deposit varies from broker to broker. Some brokers have a minimum of $10,000; others let you open an account for as little as $500. Once in a while you may see a broker offering cash accounts with no minimum deposit, usually as part of a promotion. Qualifying for a cash account is usually easy.

With a cash account, your money has to be deposited in the account before the closing (or settlement) date for any trade you make. The closing occurs three business days after the date you make the trade (the *date of execution*). You may be required to have the money in the account even before the date of execution. See Chapter 4 for details on these and other important dates.

In other words, if you call your broker on Monday, October 10, and order 50 shares of CashLess Corp. at $20 per share, then on Thursday, October 13, you better have $1,000 in cash sitting in your account (plus commission). Otherwise, the purchase doesn't go through.

In addition, ask the broker how long it takes deposited cash (such as a check) to be available for investing. Some brokers put a hold on checks for up to ten business days (or longer), regardless of how soon that check clears your account.

See whether your broker will pay you interest on the uninvested cash in your brokerage account. Some brokers offer a service in which uninvested money earns money market rates, and you can even choose between a regular money market account and a tax-free municipal money market account.

Margin accounts

A *margin account* (also called a *Type 2 account*) allows you to borrow money against the securities in the account to buy more stock. Because you can borrow in a margin account, you have to be qualified and approved by the broker. After you're approved, this newfound credit gives you more leverage so you can buy more stock or do short selling. (You can read more about buying on margin and short selling in Chapter 9.)

For stock trading, the margin limit is 50 percent. For example, if you plan to buy $10,000 worth of stock on margin, you need at least $5,000 in cash (or securities owned) sitting in your account. The interest rate you pay varies depending on the broker, but most brokers generally charge a rate that's several points higher than their own borrowing rate.

Why use margin? Margin is to stocks what a mortgage is to buying real estate. You can buy real estate with all cash, but using borrowed funds often makes sense because you may not have enough money to make a 100 percent cash purchase, or you may just prefer not to pay all cash. With margin, you can, for example, buy $10,000 worth of stock with as little as $5,000. The balance of the stock purchase is acquired using a loan (margin) from the brokerage firm.

Personally, I'm not a big fan of margin, and I use it sparingly. Margin is a form of leverage that can work out fine if you're correct but can be very dangerous if the market moves against you. It's best applied with stocks that are generally stable and dividend-paying. That way, the dividends help pay off the margin interest.

Options accounts

An *options account* (also referred to as a *Type 3 account*) gives you all the capabilities of a margin account (which in turn also gives you the capabilities of a cash account) plus the ability to trade options on stocks and stock indexes. To upgrade your margin account to an options account, the broker usually asks you to sign a statement that you're knowledgeable about options and familiar with the risks associated with them.

Options can be a very effective addition to a stock investor's array of wealth-building investment tools. I personally love to use options (as do my clients and students), and I think they can be a great tool in your wealth-building arsenal.

Judge Brokers' Advice

In recent years, Americans have become enamored with a new sport: the rating of stocks by brokers on TV financial shows. Some stocks have been known to jump significantly right after an influential analyst issues a buy recommendation. However, most investors should be very wary when analysts, especially the glib ones on TV, make a recommendation. It's often just showbiz. The following sections define basic broker recommendations and list a few important considerations for evaluating them.

Understand basic recommendations

Brokers issue their recommendations (advice) as a general idea of how much regard they have for a particular stock. The following list presents the basic recommendations (or ratings) and what they mean to you:

- *Strong buy* **and** *buy:* The analyst loves this pick, and you would be very wise to get a bunch of shares. The thing to keep in mind, however, is that *buy* recommendations are probably the most common because (let's face it) brokers sell stocks.

- *Accumulate* **and** *market perform:* An analyst who issues these types of recommendations is positive, yet unexcited, about the pick. For some brokers, *accumulate* is considered a *buy* recommendation.

- *Hold* **or** *neutral:* Analysts use this language when their backs are to the wall, but they still don't want to say, "Sell!"

- *Sell:* Many analysts should have issued this recommendation during the bear markets of 2000–2002 and 2008 but didn't. What a shame. So many investors lost money because some analysts were too nice (or biased?) or just afraid to be honest, sound the alarm, and urge people to sell.

Ask a few important questions

You want to view recommendations from analysts with a healthy dose of reality. Analysts have biases because their employment depends on the very companies that are being presented. What investors need to listen to when a broker talks up a stock is the reasoning behind the recommendation. In other words, why is the broker making this recommendation?

Keep in mind that analysts' recommendations can play a useful role in your personal stock investing research. If you find a great stock and *then* you hear analysts give glowing reports on the same stock, you're on the right track. Here are some questions and points to keep in mind:

- **How does the analyst arrive at a rating?** The analyst's approach to evaluating a stock can help you round out your research as you consult other sources such as newsletters and independent advisory services.

- **What analytical approach is the analyst using?** Some analysts use *fundamental analysis* (see Chapter 6) — looking at the company's financial condition and factors related to its success, such as its standing within the industry and the overall market. Other analysts use *technical analysis* — looking at the company's stock price history and judging past stock price movements to derive some insight regarding the stock's future price movement. Many analysts use a combination of the two. Is this analyst's approach similar to your approach or to those of sources that you respect or admire?

- **What is the analyst's track record?** Has the analyst had a consistently good record through both bull and bear markets? Major financial publications, such as *Barron's* and *Hulbert Financial Digest*, and websites, such as MarketWatch.com, regularly track recommendations from well-known analysts and stock pickers.

- **How does the analyst treat important aspects of the company's performance, such as sales and earnings?** The essence of a healthy company is growing sales and earnings coupled with strong assets and low debt. (See Chapter 6 for more details on these topics.)

- **Is the industry that the company's in doing well?** Do the analysts give you insight on this important information? A strong company in a weak industry can't stay strong for long. The right industry is a critical part of the stock selection process (for more information, see Chapter 7).

- **What research sources does the analyst cite?** Does the analyst quote the federal government or industry trade

_____

_____

_____

groups to support her thesis? These sources are important because they help give a more complete picture regarding the company's prospects for success. Imagine that you decide on the stock of a strong company. What if the federal government (through agencies like the SEC) is penalizing the company for fraudulent activity? Or what if the company's industry is shrinking or has ceased to grow (making it tougher for the company to continue growing)? The astute investor looks at a variety of sources before buying stock.

- **Does the company that's being recommended have any ties to the analyst or the analyst's firm?** During 2000–2002, the financial industry got bad publicity because many analysts gave positive recommendations on stocks of companies that were doing business with the very firms that employed those analysts. This conflict of interest is probably the biggest reason that analysts were so wrong in their recommendations during that period. Ask your broker to disclose any conflict of interest. Additionally, brokers are required to disclose whether their firm is involved with a particular stock as a "market maker" or in another capacity (such as being its investment banker).

6

Using Basic Accounting to Choose Winning Stocks

This chapter takes the mystery out of the numbers behind a stock. The most tried-and-true method for picking a good stock starts with picking a good company. Picking a company means looking at its products, services, industry, and financial strength. Understanding the basics behind the numbers can save your portfolio.

Recognize Value

If you pick a stock based on the value of the underlying company that issues it, you're a *value investor* — an investor who looks at a company's value to judge whether you can purchase the stock at a good price. Companies have value the same way many things have value, and there's a fair price to buy them at, too. Take eggs, for example. You can eat them and have a tasty treat while getting nutrition as well. But would you buy an egg for $1,000? Of course not. But what if you could buy an egg for 5 cents? At that point, it has value *and* a good price. This kind of deal is a value investor's dream.

Value investors analyze a company's *fundamentals* (earnings, assets, net worth, and so on) to see whether the information justifies purchasing the stock. They see whether the stock price is low relative to these verifiable, quantifiable factors. Therefore, value investors use *fundamental analysis*, whereas other investors may use technical analysis. *Technical analysis* looks at stock charts and statistical data, such as trading volume and historical stock prices. Some investors use a combination of both strategies.

History has shown that the most successful long-term investors have typically been value investors using fundamental analysis as their primary investing approach. The following sections describe different kinds of value and explain how to spot a company's value in several places.

Different types of value

Value is the essence of good stock-picking. You can measure value in different ways, so you need to know the differences and understand the impact that value has on your investment decisions.

Market value

When you hear someone quoting a stock at $47 per share, that price reflects the stock's market value. The total market valuation of a company's stock is also referred to as its *market cap* or *market capitalization*. To determine a company's market cap, you use the following formula: Market capitalization equals share price multiplied by number of shares outstanding.

_____

_____

_____

If Bolshevik Corp.'s stock is $35 per share and it has 10 million shares outstanding (or shares available for purchase), its market cap is $350 million. Granted, $350 million may sound like a lot of money, but Bolshevik Corp. is considered a small cap stock.

Millions of investors buying and selling directly and through intermediaries such as mutual funds determine the market value of any particular stock. If the market perceives that the company is desirable, investor demand for the company's stock pushes up the share price.

The problem with market valuation is that it's not always a good indicator of a good investment. Plenty of companies have had astronomical market values, yet they've proven to be very risky investments. Because market value is a direct result of buying and selling by stock investors, it can be a fleeting thing. This precariousness is why investors must understand the company behind the stock price.

Book value and intrinsic value

Book value (also referred to as *accounting value*) looks at a company from a balance sheet perspective (assets minus liabilities equals net worth, or *stockholders' equity*). It's a way of judging a firm by its net worth to see whether the stock's market value is reasonable compared to the company's intrinsic value. *Intrinsic value* is tied to what the market price of a company's assets — both *tangible* (such as equipment) and *intangible* (such as patents) — would be if they were sold.

Generally, market value tends to be higher than book value. If market value is substantially higher than book value, the value investor becomes more reluctant to buy that particular stock because it's overvalued. The closer the stock's market capitalization is to the book value, the safer the investment.

I like to be cautious with a stock whose market value is more than twice its book value. If the market value is $1 billion or more and the book value is $500 million or less, that's a good indicator that the business may be *overvalued,* or valued at a higher price than its book value and ability to generate a profit. Just understand that the farther the market value is from the company's book value, the more you'll pay for the company's real potential value. And the more you pay for the company's real value, the greater the risk that the company's market value (the stock price, that is) can decrease.

Sales value and earnings value

A company's intrinsic value is directly tied to its ability to make money. For this reason, many analysts like to value stocks from the perspective of the company's income statement. Two common barometers of value are expressed in ratios: the price to sales ratio (PSR) and the price-to-earnings (P/E) ratio. In both instances, the price is a reference to the company's market value (as reflected in its share price). Sales and earnings are references to the firm's ability to make money. These two ratios are covered more fully later in this chapter.

The closer the market value is to the company's intrinsic value, the better. And, of course, if the market value is lower than the company's intrinsic value, you have a potential bargain worthy of a closer look. Part of looking closer means examining the company's income statement (discussed later in this chapter), also called the *profit and loss statement*, or simply the *P&L*. A low price to sales ratio is 1, a medium PSR is between 1 and 2, and a high PSR is 3 or higher.

Put the pieces together

When you look at a company from a value-oriented perspective, here are some important items to consider (see the later section "Account for Value" for more):

- **The balance sheet, to figure out the company's net worth:** A value investor doesn't buy a company's stock because it's cheap; she buys it because it's *undervalued* (the company is worth more than the price its stock reflects — its market value is as close as possible to its book value).

- **The income statement, to figure out the company's profitability:** A company may be undervalued from a comparison of the book value and the market value, but that doesn't mean it's a screaming buy. For example, what if you find out that a company is in trouble and losing money this year? Do you buy its stock then? No, you don't. Why invest in the stock of a losing company? (If you do, you aren't investing — you're gambling or speculating.) The heart of a firm's value, besides its net worth, is its ability to generate profit.

_____

_____

_____

- **Ratios that let you analyze just how well (or not so well) the company is doing:** Value investors basically look for a bargain. They generally don't look at companies that everyone is talking about; by that point, the stock of those companies ceases to be a bargain. The value investor searches for a stock that will eventually be discovered by the market and then watches as the stock price goes up. But before you bother digging into the fundamentals to find that bargain, make sure the company is making money.

The more ways that you can look at a company and see value, the better:

- **Examine the P/E ratio.** Does the company have one? (This question may sound strange, but if the company is losing money, it may not have one.) Does the P/E ratio look reasonable, or is it in triple-digit territory?
- **Check out the debt load.** Next, look at the company's *debt load* (the total amount of liabilities). Is it less than the company's equity? Are sales healthy and increasing from the prior year? Does the firm compare favorably in these categories versus other companies in the same industry?

- **Think in terms of 10s.** Simplicity to me is best. You'll notice that the number 10 comes up frequently as I measure a company's performance, juxtaposing all the numbers that you need to be aware of. If net income is rising by 10 percent or more, that's fine. If the company is in the top 10 percent of its industry, that's great. If the industry is growing by 10 percent or better (sales and so on), that's terrific. If sales are up 10 percent or more from the prior year, that's wonderful.

Does every company/industry have to neatly fit these criteria? No. But it doesn't hurt you to be picky. You need to find only a handful of stocks from thousands of choices.

Value investors can find thousands of companies that have value, but they can probably buy only a handful at a truly good price. The number of stocks that can be bought at a good price is relative to the market. In mature *bull markets* (markets in a prolonged period of rising prices), a good price is hard to find because most stocks have probably seen significant price increases, but in *bear markets* (markets in a prolonged period of falling prices), good companies at bargain prices are easier to come by.

Account for Value

Stock investors need some rudimentary knowledge of accounting to round out their stock-picking prowess and to be sure that they're getting a good value for their investment dollars. Accounting is the language of business. If you don't understand basic accounting, you'll have difficulty being a successful investor. Investing without accounting knowledge is like traveling without a map. However, if you can run a household budget, using accounting analysis to evaluate stocks is easier than you think.

Websites such as www.nasdaq.com can give you the most recent balance sheets and income statements of most public companies. You can find out more about public information and company research in Chapter 4.

The balance sheet

A company's balance sheet gives you a financial snapshot of what the company looks like in terms of the following equation: assets minus liabilities equals net worth (or net equity).

Answer a few balance sheet questions

Analyze the following items that you find on the balance sheet:

- **Total assets:** Have they increased from the prior year? If not, was it because of the sale of an asset or a write-off (uncollectable accounts receivable, for example)?

- **Financial assets:** In recent years, many companies (especially banks and brokerage firms) had questionable financial assets (such as subprime mortgages) that went bad, and they had to write them off as unrecoverable losses. Does the company you're analyzing have a large exposure to financial assets that are low-quality (and hence, risky) debt?

- **Inventory:** Is inventory higher or lower than last year? If sales are flat but inventory is growing, that may be a problem.

- **Debt:** Debt is the biggest weakness on the corporate balance sheet. Make sure that debt isn't a growing item and that it's under control. In recent years, debt has become a huge problem.

- **Derivatives:** A *derivative* is a speculative and complex financial instrument that doesn't constitute ownership of an asset (such as a stock, bond, or commodity) but is a promise to convey ownership. Some derivatives are quite acceptable because they're used as protective or hedging vehicles (this use isn't my primary concern). However, they're frequently used to generate income and can then carry risks that can increase liabilities. Standard options and futures are examples of derivatives on a regulated exchange, but the derivatives I'm talking about here are a different animal and in an unregulated part of the financial world. They have a book value exceeding $600 trillion and can easily devastate a company, sector, or market (as the credit crisis of 2008 showed).

Find out whether the company dabbles in these complicated, dicey, leveraged financial instruments. Find out (from the company's 10K report) whether it has derivatives and, if so, the total amount. Having derivatives that are valued higher than the company's net equity may cause tremendous problems.

- **Equity:** *Equity* is the company's net worth (what's left if all assets are used to pay off all company debts). The stockholders' equity should be increasing steadily by at least 10 percent per year. If not, find out why.

_____

_____

_____

Table 6-1 shows you a brief example of a balance sheet.

Assets (What the Company Owns)	Amount
1. Cash and inventory	$5,000
2. Equipment and other assets	$7,000
3. TOTAL ASSETS (Item 1 plus Item 2)	$12,000
Liabilities (What the Company Owes)	**Amount**
4. Short-term debt	$1,500
5. Other debt	$2,500
6. TOTAL LIABILITIES (Item 4 plus Item 5)	$4,000
7. NET EQUITY (Item 3 minus Item 6)	$8,000

Table 6-1: *XYZ Balance Sheet — December 31, 2017*

By looking at a company's balance sheet, you can address the following questions:

- **What does the company own (assets)?** The company can own assets, which can be financial, tangible, and/or intangible. An *asset* is anything that has value or that can be converted to or sold for cash. Financial assets can be cash, investments (such as stocks or bonds of other companies), or accounts receivable. Assets can be tangible items such as inventory, equipment, and/or buildings. They can also be intangible things such as licenses, trademarks, or copyrights.

_____

_____

_____

- **What does the company owe (liabilities)?** A *liability* is anything of value that the company must ultimately pay someone else for. Liabilities can be invoices (accounts payable) or short-term or long-term debt.

- **What is the company's net equity (net worth)?** After you subtract the liabilities from the assets, the remainder is called *net worth, net equity,* or *net stockholders' equity*. This number is critical when calculating a company's book value.

Assess a company's financial strength over time

Compare a company's balance sheet at a recent point in time to a past time. You should do this comparative analysis with all the key items on the balance sheet, listed in the preceding section, to see the company's progress (or lack thereof). Is it growing its assets and/or shrinking its debt? Is the company's net worth growing? Has it grown by at least 10 percent since a year ago? All too often, investors stop doing their homework after they make an initial investment. You should continue to look at the firm's numbers regularly so you can be ahead of the curve. If the business starts having problems, you can get out

_____

_____

_____

before the rest of the market starts getting out (which causes the stock price to fall).

To judge the financial strength of a company, ask yourself the following questions:

- **Are the company's assets greater in value than they were three months ago, a year ago, or two years ago?** Compare current asset size to the most recent two years to make sure that the company is growing in size and financial strength.

- **How do the individual items compare with prior periods?** Some particular assets that you want to take note of are cash, inventory, and accounts receivable. Are liabilities such as accounts payable and debt about the same, lower, or higher compared to prior periods? Are they growing at a similar, faster, or slower rate than the company's assets? Debt that rises faster and higher than items on the other side of the balance sheet is a warning sign of pending financial problems.

- **Is the company's net worth or equity greater than the preceding year? And is that year's equity greater than the year before?** In a healthy company, the net worth is constantly rising. As a general rule, in good economic times, net worth should be at least 10 percent higher than the preceding year. In tough economic times (such as a recession), 5 percent is acceptable. Seeing the net worth grow at a rate of 15 percent or higher is great.

The income statement

To find out a company's profit, check out the firm's income statement. It reports a simple accounting equation that you probably already know: sales minus expenses equals net profit (or net earnings, or net income). Look at the following figures found on the income statement:

- **Sales:** Are they increasing? If not, why not? By what percentage are sales increasing? Preferably, they should be 10 percent higher than the year before.

- **Expenses:** Do you see any unusual items? Are total expenses reported higher than the prior year, and if so, by how much? If the total is significantly higher, why? A company with large, rising expenses will see profits suffer, which isn't good for the stock price.

- **Research and development (R&D):** How much is the company spending on R&D? Companies that rely on new product development (such as pharmaceuticals or biotech firms) should spend at least as much as they did the year before (preferably more) because new products mean future earnings and growth.

- **Earnings:** This figure reflects the bottom line. Are total earnings higher than the year before? How about earnings from operations (leaving out expenses such as taxes and interest)? Out of all the numbers in the financial statements, earnings have the greatest single impact on the company's stock price.

Table 6-2 shows you a brief example of an income statement.

Total Sales (Or Revenue)	Amount
1. Sales of products	$11,000
2. Sales of services	$3,000
3. TOTAL SALES (Item 1 plus Item 2)	$14,000
Expenses	**Amount**
4. Marketing and promotion	$2,000
5. Payroll costs	$9,000
6. Other costs	$1,500
7. TOTAL EXPENSES (Item 4 plus Item 5 plus Item 6)	$12,500
8. NET INCOME (Item 3 minus Item 7) (In this case, it's a net profit)	$1,500

Table 6-2: *XYZ Income Statement for Year Ending December 31, 2017*

Looking at the income statement, an investor can try to answer the following questions:

- **What sales did the company make?** Businesses sell products and services that generate revenue (known as *sales* or *gross sales*). Sales also are referred to as the *top line.*

- **What expenses did the company incur?** In generating sales, companies pay expenses such as payroll, utilities, advertising, administration, and so on.

- **What is the net profit?** Also called *net earnings* or *net income,* net profit is the *bottom line.* After paying for all expenses, what profit did the company make?

The information you glean should give you a strong idea about a firm's current financial strength and whether it's successfully increasing sales, holding down expenses, and ultimately maintaining profitability. You can find out more about sales, expenses, and profits in the sections that follow.

Sales

Sales refers to the money that a company receives as customers buy its goods and/or services. Analyzing a business by looking

_____

_____

_____

at its sales is called *top line analysis*. As an investor, you should take into consideration the following points about sales:

- **Sales should be increasing.** A healthy, growing company has growing sales. They should grow at least 10 percent from the prior year, and you should look at the most recent three years.

- **Core sales (sales of those products or services that the company specializes in) should be increasing.** Frequently, the sales figure has a lot of stuff lumped into it. Maybe the company sells widgets, but the core sales shouldn't include other things, such as the sale of a building or other unusual items. Isolate the firm's primary offerings and ask whether these sales are growing at a reasonable rate (such as 10 percent).

- **Does the company have odd items or odd ways of calculating sales?** Say you find out that Suspicious Sales Inc. (SSI) had annual sales of $50 million, reflecting a 25 percent increase from the year before. Looks great! But what if you find out that $20 million of that sales number comes from sales made on credit that the company extended to buyers? Some companies that use this approach later have to write off losses as uncollectable debt because the customers ultimately can't pay for the goods.

If you want to get a good clue as to whether a company is artificially boosting sales, check its accounts receivable (listed in the asset section of its balance sheet). *Accounts receivable* refers to money that is owed to the company for goods that customers have purchased on credit. If you find out that sales went up by $10 million (great!) but accounts receivable went up by $20 million (uh-oh), something just isn't right. That may be a sign that the financing terms were too easy, and the company may have a problem collecting payment (especially in a recession).

Expenses

How much a company spends has a direct relationship to its profitability. If spending isn't held at a sustainable level, it may spell trouble for the business. When you look at a company's expense items, consider the following:

- **Compare expense items to the prior period.** Are expenses higher than, lower than, or about the same as those from the prior period? If the difference is significant, you should see commensurate benefits elsewhere. In other words, if overall expenses are 10 percent higher compared to the prior period, are sales at least 10 percent more during the same period?

- **Are some expenses too high?** Look at the individual expense items. Are they significantly higher than the year before? If so, why?

- **Have any unusual items been expensed?** An unusual expense isn't necessarily a negative. Expenses may be higher than usual if a company writes off uncollectable accounts receivable as a bad debt expense. Doing so inflates the total expenses and subsequently results in lower earnings. Pay attention to nonrecurring charges that show up on the income statement and determine whether they make sense.

Profit

Earnings or profit is the single most important item on the income statement. When a company makes a profit, it's usually reported as earnings per share (EPS). So if you hear that XYZ Corporation beat last quarter's earnings by a penny, here's how to translate that news. Suppose that the company made

_____

_____

_____

$1 per share this quarter and 99 cents per share last quarter. If that company had 100 million shares of stock outstanding, its profit this quarter is $100 million (the EPS times the number of shares outstanding), which is $1 million more than it made in the prior quarter ($1 million is 1 cent per share times 100 million shares).

> Don't simply look at current earnings as an isolated figure. Always compare current earnings to earnings in past periods (usually a year). For example, if you're looking at a retailer's fourth-quarter results, don't compare them with the retailer's third-quarter outcome. What if the company usually does well during the December holidays but poorly in the fall? In that case, you don't get a fair comparison.

A strong company should show consistent earnings growth from the period before (such as the prior year or the same quarter from the prior year), and you should check the period before that, too, so that you can determine whether earnings are consistently rising over time. Earnings growth is an important barometer of the company's potential growth and bodes well for the stock price.

When you look at earnings, here are some things to consider:

- **Total earnings:** This item is the most watched. Total earnings should grow year to year by at least 10 percent.

- **Operational earnings:** Break down the total earnings and look at a key subset — that portion of earnings derived from the company's core activity. Is the company continuing to make money from its primary goods and services?

- **Nonrecurring items:** Are earnings higher (or lower) than usual or than expected, and if so, why? Frequently, the difference results from items such as the sale of an asset or a large depreciation write-off.

Ten percent is a good number because it's easy to calculate and it's a good benchmark. However, 5 percent isn't unacceptable if you're talking about tough times, such as a recession. Obviously, if sales, earnings, and/or net worth are hitting or surpassing 15 percent, that's great.

Ratios

A *ratio* is a helpful numerical tool that you can use to find out the relationship between two or more figures found in a company's financial data. A ratio can add meaning to a number or put it in perspective. Ratios sound complicated, but they're easier to understand than you may think.

Two key ratios to be aware of are

- Price-to-earnings (P/E) ratio

- Price to sales ratio (PSR)

Use stock screening tools available for free on the Internet to do your research. A *stock screening tool* lets you plug in numbers, such as sales or earnings, and ratios, such as the P/E ratio or the debt to equity ratio, and then up come stocks that fit your criteria. Many brokers have them at their websites (such as Charles Schwab at www.schwab.com and E*TRADE at www.etrade.com). You can also find tools at Yahoo! Finance (finance.yahoo.com), Bloomberg (www.bloomberg.com), Nasdaq (www.nasdaq.com), and MarketWatch (www.marketwatch.com).

The P/E ratio

The *price-to-earnings (P/E) ratio* is very important in analyzing a potential stock investment because it's one of the most widely regarded barometers of a company's value, and it's usually reported along with the company's stock price in the financial page listing. The major significance of the P/E ratio is that it establishes a direct relationship between the bottom line of a company's operations — the earnings (or net profit) — and the stock price.

The *P* in P/E stands for the stock's current price. The *E* is for earnings per share (typically the most recent 12 months of earnings). The P/E ratio is also referred to as the *earnings multiple* or just *multiple*.

You calculate the P/E ratio by dividing the price of the stock by the earnings per share. If the price of a single share of stock is $10 and the earnings (on a per-share basis) are $1, then the P/E is 10. If the stock price goes to $35 per share and the earnings are unchanged, then the P/E is 35. Basically, the higher the P/E, the more you pay for the company's earnings.

Why would you buy stock in one company with a relatively high P/E ratio instead of investing in another company with a lower P/E ratio? Keep in mind that investors buy stocks based on expectations. They may bid up the price of the stock (subsequently raising the stock's P/E ratio) because they feel that the company will have increased earnings in the near future. Perhaps they feel that the company has great potential (a pending new invention or lucrative business deal) that will eventually make it more profitable. More profitability in turn has a beneficial impact on the firm's stock price. The danger with a high P/E is that if the company doesn't achieve the hoped-for results, the stock price can fall.

You should look at two types of P/E ratios to get a balanced picture of the company's value:

- **Trailing P/E:** This P/E is the most frequently quoted because it deals with existing data. The trailing P/E uses the most recent 12 months of earnings in its calculation.

- **Forward P/E:** This P/E is based on projections or expectations of earnings in the coming 12-month period. It's considered an estimate that may or may not prove to be accurate.

Say that you want to buy a business and I'm selling a business. You come to me and say, "What do you have to offer?" I say, "I operate a retail business downtown that sells spatulas. The business nets a cool $2,000 profit per year." You say, "Uh, okay, what's the asking price for the business?" I reply, "You can have it for only $1 million! What do you say?"

The business is way overvalued (too expensive for what you're getting in return for your investment dollars). The million dollars would generate a better rate of return elsewhere and probably with less risk. As for the business, the P/E ratio of 500 ($1 million divided by $2,000) is outrageous. This is definitely a case of an overvalued company — and a lousy investment.

What if I offered the business for $12,000? The P/E ratio is a more reasonable 6 ($12,000 divided by $2,000). In other words, the business pays for itself in about 6 years (versus 500 years in the prior example).

Looking at the P/E ratio offers a shortcut for investors asking the question, "Is this stock overvalued?" As a general rule, the lower the P/E, the safer (or more conservative) the stock is. The reverse is more noteworthy: The higher the P/E, the greater the risk.

When someone refers to a P/E as high or low, you have to ask the question, "Compared to what?" A P/E of 30 is considered very high for a large cap electric utility but quite reasonable for a small cap, high-technology firm. Keep in mind that phrases such as *large cap* and *small cap* are just a reference to the company's market value or size. *Cap* is short for *capitalization* (the total number of shares of stock outstanding multiplied by the share price).

The following points can help you evaluate P/E ratios:

- **Compare a company's P/E ratio with its industry.** Electric utility industry stocks, for example, generally have a P/E that hovers in the 9–14 range. Therefore, an electric utility with a P/E of 45 indicates that something is wrong with that utility. (I touch on sectors and industries in Chapter 7.)

- **Compare a company's P/E with the general market.** If you're looking at a small cap stock on the Nasdaq that has a P/E of 100 and the average P/E for established companies on the Nasdaq is 40, find out why. You should also compare the stock's P/E ratio with the P/E ratio for major indexes such as the Dow Jones Industrial Average (DJIA), the Standard & Poor's 500 (S&P 500), and the Nasdaq Composite. Stock indexes are useful for getting the big picture, and I include them in Chapter 8.

- **Compare a company's current P/E with recent periods** (such as this year versus last year). If it currently has a P/E ratio of 20 and it previously had a P/E ratio of 30, you know that either the stock price has declined or that earnings have risen. In this case, the stock is less likely to fall. That bodes well for the stock.

- **Low P/E ratios aren't necessarily a sign of a bargain,** but if you're looking at a stock for many other reasons that seem positive (solid sales, strong industry, and so on) and it also has a low P/E, that's a good sign.

- **High P/E ratios aren't necessarily bad,** but they do mean that you should investigate further. If a company is weak and the industry is shaky, heed the high P/E as a warning sign. Frequently, a high P/E ratio means that investors have bid up a stock price, anticipating future income. The problem is that if the anticipated income doesn't materialize, the stock price can fall.

- **Watch out for a stock that doesn't have a P/E ratio.** In other words, it may have a price (the *P*), but it doesn't have earnings (the *E*). No earnings means no P/E, meaning that you're better off avoiding the stock.

The PSR

The *price to sales ratio (PSR)* is a company's stock price divided by its sales. Because the sales number is rarely expressed as a per-share figure, it's easier to divide a company's total market value (explained earlier in this chapter) by its total sales for the last 12 months.

As a general rule, stock trading at a PSR of 1 or less is a reasonably priced stock worthy of your attention. Say that a company has sales of $1 billion and the stock has a total market value of $950 million. In that case, the PSR is 0.95. In other words, you can buy $1 of the company's sales for only 95 cents. All things being equal, that stock may be a bargain.

Compare the company's PSR with other companies in the same industry, along with the industry average, so that you get a better idea of the company's relative value.

7

Emerging Sector and Industry Opportunities

A successful long-term investor looks at an industry (or a sector) just as carefully as he looks at an individual stock. Luckily, choosing a winning industry to invest in is easier than choosing individual stocks, as this chapter explains.

The Difference between a Sector and an Industry

A *sector* is simply a group of interrelated industries. An *industry* is typically a category of business that performs a more precise activity; you can call an industry a *subsector.* Investing in a sector and investing in an industry can mean different things for the investor. The result of your investment performance can also be very different.

Healthcare is an example of a sector that has different industries. The sector of healthcare includes such industries as pharmaceuticals, drug retailers, health insurance, hospitals, medical equipment manufacturers, and so on.

Healthcare is actually a good example of why you should know the distinction between a sector and an industry. Within a given sector (like healthcare), you have industries that behave differently during the same economic conditions. Some industries are cyclical (like medical equipment manufacturers), whereas some are defensive (like drug retailers). In a bad economy, cyclicals tend to go down while defensive stocks generally hold their value. In a booming economy, cyclicals do very well while defensive stocks tend to lag behind. (Find out more about cyclical and defensive industries later in this chapter.)

Interrogate the Sectors and Industries

Your common sense is important in choosing sectors and industries with winning stocks. This section explores questions to ask when you're choosing a sector or industry.

Which category does the industry fall into?

Most industries can be placed in one of two categories: cyclical or defensive. These categories generally translate into what society wants and what it needs. Society buys what it *wants* when times are good and holds off when times are bad. It buys what it *needs* in both good and bad times.

Cyclical industries

Cyclical industries are industries whose fortunes rise and fall with the economy's rise and fall. In other words, if the economy and the stock market are doing well, consumers and investors are confident and tend to spend and invest more money than usual, so cyclical industries tend to do well. Real estate and automobiles are great examples of cyclical industries.

Think about your behavior as a consumer, and you get a revealing clue into the thinking of millions of consumers. When you (and millions of others) feel good about your career, finances, and future, you have a greater tendency to buy more (and/or more expensive) stuff. Also, people take on more debt because they feel confident that they can pay it back. In light of this behavior, what industries do you think would do well?

The same point holds for business spending. When businesses think that economic times are good and foresee continuing good times, they tend to spend more money on large purchases such as new equipment or technology. They think that when they're doing well and are flush with financial success, it's a good idea to reinvest that money in the business to increase future success.

Defensive industries

Defensive industries produce goods and services that are needed no matter what's happening in the economy. Think about what millions of people buy no matter how bad the economy gets. A good example is food — people still need to eat regardless of good or bad times. Other examples of defensive industries are utilities and healthcare.

In bad economic times, defensive stocks tend to do better than cyclical stocks. However, when times are good, cyclical stocks tend to do better than defensive stocks. Defensive stocks don't do as well in good times because people don't necessarily eat twice as much or use up more electricity.

The growth of defensive stocks relies on two factors:

- **Population growth:** As more and more consumers are born, more people become available to buy.
- **New markets:** A company can grow by seeking out new groups of consumers to buy its products and services.

 One way to invest in a particular industry is to take advantage of exchange-traded funds (ETFs). ETFs are structured much like mutual funds but are fixed portfolios that trade like a stock. If you find a winning industry but you can't find a winning stock (or don't want to bother with the necessary research), ETFs are a great consideration. You can find out more about ETFs by turning to Chapter 8.

Is the sector growing?

The saying "the trend is your friend" applies when choosing a sector in which to invest, as long as the trend is an upward one. If you look at three different stocks that are equal in every significant way but you find that one stock is in a sector growing 15 percent per year while the other two stocks are in sectors that have either little growth or are shrinking, which stock would you choose?

 To judge how well a sector or industry is doing, various information sources monitor all the sectors and industries and measure their progress. Some reliable sources include

- MarketWatch (www.marketwatch.com)
- Standard & Poor's (www.standardandpoors.com)
- D&B Hoovers (www.hoovers.com)
- Yahoo! Finance (finance.yahoo.com)
- *The Wall Street Journal* (www.wsj.com)

Are the sector's products or services in demand?

Look at the products and services that the sector or industry provides. Do they look like things that society will continue to want? Are there products and services on the horizon that could replace them? What does the foreseeable future look like for the sector?

When evaluating future demand, look for a *sunrise industry* — one that's new or emerging or has promising appeal for the future. Good examples of sunrise industries in recent years are biotech and Internet companies. In contrast, a *sunset industry* is one that's either declining or has little potential for growth. For example, you probably shouldn't invest in the DVD manufacturing industry because demand is shifting toward digital delivery instead. Owning stock in a strong, profitable company in a sunrise industry is obviously the most desirable choice.

Current research unveils the following megatrends:

- **The aging of the United States:** More senior citizens than ever before are living in the United States. Healthcare and financial services that touch on eldercare or financial concerns of the elderly will prosper.

- **Advances in high technology:** Internet, telecom, medical, and biotechnology innovations will continue.

- **Security concerns:** Terrorism, international tensions, and security issues on a personal level mean more

attention for national defense, homeland security, and
related matters.

- **Energy challenges:** Traditional and nontraditional
sources of energy (such as solar, fuel cells, and so on)
will demand society's attention as it transitions from
fossil fuels to new forms of energy.

 One of my favorite resources for anticipating megatrends is Gerald Celente and his Trends Journal (www.
trendsresearch.com).

What does the industry's growth rely on?

An industry doesn't exist in a vacuum. External factors weigh
heavily on its ability to survive and thrive. Does the industry
rely on an established megatrend? Then it will probably be
strong for a while. Does it rely on factors that are losing rel-
evance? Then it may begin to decline soon. Technological and
demographic changes are other factors that may contribute to
an industry's growth or fall.

Keep in mind that a sector will either continue to grow,
shrink, or be level, but individual industries can grow, shrink,
or even be on track to disappear. If a sector is expanding, you

may see new industries emerge. For example, the graying of the United States is an established megatrend. As millions of Americans climb into their later years, profitable opportunities await companies that are prepared to cater to them. Perhaps an industry (subsector) offers great new medical products for senior citizens. What are the prospects for growth?

Is the industry dependent on another industry?

Industries frequently are intertwined. When one industry suffers, you may find it helpful to understand which industries will subsequently suffer. The reverse can also be true — when one industry is doing well, other industries may reap the benefits.

In either case, if the stock you choose is in an industry that's highly dependent on other industries, you should know about it. If you're considering stocks of resort companies and you see the headlines blaring, "Airlines losing money as public stops flying," what do you do? This type of question forces you to think logically and consider cause and effect. Logic and common sense are powerful tools that frequently trump all the number-crunching performed by analysts.

_____

_____

_____

Who are the leading companies in the industry?

After you choose the industry, what types of companies do you want to invest in? There are two basic types:

- **Established leaders:** These companies are considered industry leaders or have a large share of the market. Investing in these companies is the safer way to go; what better choice for novice investors than companies that have already proven themselves?

- **Innovators:** If the industry is hot and you want to be more aggressive in your approach, investigate companies that offer new products, patents, or technologies. These companies may be smaller but have a greater potential for growth in a proven industry.

Is the industry a target of government action?

You need to know whether the government is targeting an industry because intervention by politicians and bureaucrats can have an impact on an industry's economic situation.

Investors need to take heed when political "noise" starts coming out about a particular industry. An industry can be hurt by either direct government intervention or the threat of it. Intervention can take the form of lawsuits, investigations, taxes, regulations, or sometimes an outright ban. In any case, being on the wrong end of government intervention is the greatest external threat to a company's survival.

Sometimes, government action helps an industry. Generally, beneficial action takes two forms:

- **Deregulation and/or tax decreases:** Government sometimes reduces burdens on an industry. During the late 1990s, government deregulation led the way to more innovation in telecommunications. This trend laid the groundwork for more innovation and growth in the Internet and expansion of cellphone service.

- **Direct funding:** Government has the power to steer taxpayer money toward business. In recent years, federal and state governments have provided tax credits and other incentives for alternative energy such as solar power.

Key Sectors and Industries

This section highlights some sectors and industries that investors should take note of. Consider investing some of your stock portfolio in those that look promising.

Many investors can benefit from a practice referred to as *sector rotation*. The idea is that you shift money from one sector to another based on current or expectant economic conditions. If the economy is doing poorly or if the outlook appears bearish, you shift to defensive sectors such as consumer staples and utilities. If the economy is doing well, you shift money to cyclicals such as technology and base materials. Use the resources in the earlier section "Is the sector growing?" to find out more.

Real estate

Real estate is a cyclical *bellwether industry* — one that has a great effect on many other industries that may be dependent on it. Real estate is looked at as a key component of economic health because so many other industries — including building materials, mortgages, household appliances, and contract labor services — are tied to it. A booming real estate industry bodes well for much of the economy.

Housing starts are one way to measure real estate activity. This data is an important leading indicator of health in the industry. Housing starts indicate new construction, which means more business for related industries.

Keep an eye on the real estate industry for negative news that could be bearish for the economy and the stock market. Because real estate is purchased with mortgage money, investors and analysts watch the mortgage market for trouble signs such as rising delinquencies and foreclosures. These statistics serve as a warning for general economic weakness.

The real estate industry soared during 2000–2006 and cratered during 2007–2012. As I write this, the real estate industry is stabilizing after several very difficult years. As you read this, the industry may very well start its path to normalization.

Automotive

Cars are big-ticket items and another barometer of people's economic well-being — people buy new cars when they're doing well financially (or at least perceive that they're doing well). A rise in car sales is usually considered to be a positive indicator for the economy.

Although the government has used taxpayer funds to rescue some individual companies (such as General Motors), the automotive industry is still not on a healthy track despite the fact that it had record sales in recent years. The reason is that a huge percentage of those auto sales were due to subpar or subprime debt that was eerily similar to the subprime debt from the housing bubble. Some of these auto loans were for 84 months (a seven-year auto loan), which is a bad idea for a depreciating asset that requires substantial repairs after five years of wear and tear. In other words, expect problems for the auto industry at the time of this writing.

Computers and related electronics

In recent years, technology stocks have become very popular with investors. Indeed, technology is a great sector, and its impact on the economy's present and future success can't be underestimated. The share price of technology companies can rise substantially because investors buy shares based on expectations — today's untested, unproven companies may become the Googles and Apples of tomorrow.

With the success of Apple as it has forged a path in the world of personal electronics (such as the iPhone), this area will continue to show growth as worldwide consumer demand continues to show strength. Don't lose sight of the fundamentals as this industry continues to mature.

In spite of the sector's potential, companies can still fail if customers don't embrace their products. Even in technology stocks, you still must apply the rules and guidelines about financially successful companies discussed in this book. Pick the best in a growing industry and you'll succeed over the long haul.

Financials

Banking and financial services are intrinsic parts of any economy. Debt is the most important sign of this industry for investors. If a company's debt is growing faster than the economy, you need to watch how that debt impacts stocks and mutual funds. If debt gets out of control, it can be disastrous for the economy.

As one of my favorite credit specialists, Doug Noland, points out (he writes the Credit Bubble Bulletin at www. creditbubblebulletin.blogspot.com), the amount of debt and debt-related securities have reached historic and troublesome levels. This trend means that many financial stocks are at risk if a recession hits anytime soon.

Investors should be very selective in this industry and should embrace only those lenders that are conservative in their balance sheet and are generally avoiding overexposure in areas such as international finance and derivatives.

8

Exchange-Traded Funds

Sometimes you face investing environments that make finding a winning stock difficult. Prudent stock investors should consider adding exchange-traded funds — the subject of this chapter — to their wealth-building arsenal. An *exchange-traded fund* (ETF) is basically a mutual fund that invests in a fixed basket of securities but with a few twists.

 To find out more about ETFs in general, go to websites such as www.etfdb.com and www.etfguide.com.

Compare Exchange-Traded Funds and Mutual Funds

For many folks and for many years, the only choice besides investing directly in stocks was to invest indirectly through mutual funds. After all, why buy a single stock for roughly the same few thousand dollars that you can buy a mutual fund for and get benefits such as professional management and diversification?

For small investors, mutual fund investing isn't a bad way to go. Investors participate by pooling their money with others and get professional money management in an affordable manner. But mutual funds have their downsides. Mutual fund fees, which include management fees and sales charges (referred to as *loads*), eat into gains, and investors have no choice about investments. Whatever the fund manager buys, sells, or holds on to is pretty much what the investors in the fund have to tolerate.

But now, with the advent of ETFs, investors have greater choices than ever, a scenario that sets the stage for the inevitable comparison between mutual funds and ETFs. The following sections go over the differences and similarities.

The differences

Simply stated, in a mutual fund, securities such as stocks and bonds are constantly bought, sold, and held (in other words, the fund is *actively managed*). An ETF holds similar securities, but the portfolio typically isn't actively managed. Instead, an ETF usually holds a fixed basket of securities that may reflect an index or a particular industry or sector (see Chapter 7). An *index* is a method of measuring the value of a segment of the general stock market. It's a tool used by money managers and investors to compare the performance of a particular stock to a widely accepted standard; see the later section "Indexes" for more details.

For example, an ETF that tries to reflect the S&P 500 will attempt to hold a securities portfolio that mirrors the composition of the S&P 500 as closely as possible.

Where ETFs are markedly different from mutual funds is that they can be bought and sold like stocks. In addition, you can do with ETFs what you can generally do with stocks (but can't usually do with mutual funds): You can buy in share allotments, such as 1, 50, or 100 shares or more. Mutual funds, on the other hand, are usually bought in dollar amounts, such as 1,000 or 5,000 dollars' worth. The dollar amount you can initially invest is set by the manager of the individual mutual fund.

You can put various buy/sell brokerage orders on ETFs (see Chapter 9), and many ETFs are *optionable* (meaning you may be able to buy/sell put and call options on them). Mutual funds typically aren't optionable. In addition, many ETFs are *marginable* (you can borrow against them with some limitations in your brokerage account; see Chapter 9). Mutual funds usually aren't marginable.

Sometimes an investor can readily see the great potential of a given industry or sector but is hard-pressed to get that single really good stock that can take advantage of the profit possibilities of that particular segment of the market. The great thing about an ETF is that you can make that investment very easily, knowing that if you're unsure about it, you can put in place strategies that protect you from the downside (such as stop-loss orders or trailing stops).

The similarities

Even though ETFs and mutual funds have some major differences, they do share a few similarities:

- They aren't direct investments; they're "conduits" of investing, which means that they act like a connection between the investor and the investments.

- They basically pool the money of investors and the pool becomes the "fund," which in turn invests in a portfolio of investments.

- They offer the great advantage of diversification (although they accomplish it in different ways).

- Investors don't choose what makes up the portfolio of either the ETF or the mutual fund. The ETF has a fixed basket of securities (the money manager overseeing the portfolio makes those choices), and investors can't control the choices made in a mutual fund.

Choose an Exchange-Traded Fund

Buying a stock is an investment in a particular company, but an ETF is an opportunity to invest in a block of stocks. In the same way a few mouse clicks can buy you a stock at a stock brokerage website, those same clicks can buy you virtually an entire industry or sector.

For investors who are comfortable with their own choices and do their due diligence, a winning stock is a better (albeit more aggressive) way to go. For those investors who want to make their own choices but aren't that confident about picking winning stocks, an ETF is a better way to go.

There are considerations that you should be aware of, some of which are tied more to your personal outlook and preferences than to the ETF's underlying portfolio. This section gives you info on bullish and bearish ETFs.

Picking a winning industry or sector is easier than finding a great company to invest in. ETF investing goes hand in hand with the guidance offered in Chapter 7.

Bullish ETFs

You may wake up one day and say, "I think that the stock market will do very well going forward from today," and that's just fine if you think so. Maybe your research on the general economy, financial outlook, and political considerations makes you feel happy. But you just don't know which stocks would best benefit from the good market moves yet to come. No problem. The following sections cover ETF strategies for bullish scenarios.

Major market index ETFs

Why not invest in ETFs that mirror a general major market index such as the S&P 500? ETFs such as SPY construct their portfolios to track the composition of the S&P 500 as closely as possible. It's a great way to go when the market is having a good rally. (See the later section "Indexes" for the basics.)

When the S&P 500 was battered in late 2008 and early 2009, the ETF for the S&P 500 mirrored that performance and hit the bottom in March 2009. But from that moment on and into 2015, the S&P 500 (and the ETFs that tracked it) did extraordinarily well. It paid to buck the bearish sentiment of early 2009. Of course, it did take some contrarian gumption to do so, but at least you had the benefit of the full S&P 500 stock portfolio, which at least had more diversification than a single stock or a single subsection of the market. Of course, as the S&P 500 entered the bull market of 2009–2015, bullish ETFs that mirrored the S&P 500 did very well while the ETFs that were inverse to the S&P 500 (betting on a bearish move) declined in the same period.

ETFs related to human need

Some ETFs cover industries such as water, energy, and other things that people will keep buying no matter how good or bad the economy is. A stock investor can simply put money into stocks — or in this case, ETFs — tied to human need. Such ETFs may even do better than ETFs tied to major market indexes (see the preceding section).

At the end of 2007 (mere months before the great 2008–2009 market crash), what would have happened if you had invested 50 percent of your money in an ETF that represented the S&P 500 and 50 percent in an ETF that was in consumer staples (such as food and beverage stocks)? I did such a comparison; by the end of 2015, the consumer staples ETF (for the record I used PBJ) beat out the S&P 500 ETF by more than 45 percent (not including dividends).

ETFs that include dividend-paying stocks

ETFs don't have to be tied to a specific industry or sector; they can be tied to a specific type or subcategory of stock. You can find ETFs that include high-dividend income stocks (typically 4 percent or higher) as well as ETFs that include stocks of companies that don't necessarily pay high dividends but do have a long track record of dividend increases that meet or exceed the rate of inflation.

Given these types of dividend-paying ETFs, it becomes clear which is good for what type of stock investor:

- If I were a stock investor who was currently retired, I'd choose the high-dividend stock ETF. Dividend-paying stock ETFs are generally more stable than those stock ETFs that don't pay dividends, and dividends are important for retirement income.

- If I were in "pre-retirement" (years away from retirement but planning for it), I'd choose the ETF with the stocks that had a strong record of growing the dividend payout. Those same dividend-paying stocks would grow in the short term and provide better income down the road during retirement.

Dividend-paying stocks generally fall within the criteria of human need investing because those companies tend to be large and stable, with good cash flows, giving them the ongoing wherewithal to pay good dividends.

Bearish ETFs

Most ETFs are bullish in nature because they invest in a portfolio of securities that they expect to go up in due course. But some ETFs have a bearish focus. Bearish ETFs (also called *short ETFs*) maintain a portfolio of securities and strategies designed to go the opposite way of the underlying or targeted securities. In other words, this type of ETF goes up when the underlying securities go down (and vice versa).

Take the S&P 500. If you were bullish on that index, you might choose an ETF such as SPY. However, if you were bearish on that index and wanted to seek gains by betting that it would go down, you could choose an ETF such as SH.

You can take two approaches on bearish ETFs:

- **Hoping for a downfall:** If you're speculating on a pending market crash, a bearish ETF is a good consideration. In this approach, you're actually seeking to make a profit based on your expectations. Those folks who went into bearish ETFs during early or mid-2008 made some spectacular profits during the tumultuous downfall during late 2008 and early 2009.

- **Hedging against a downfall:** A more conservative approach is to use bearish ETFs to a more moderate extent, primarily as a form of hedging, whereby the bearish ETF acts like a form of insurance in the unwelcome event of a significant market pullback or crash. I say "unwelcome" because you're not hoping for a crash; you're trying to protect yourself with a modest form of diversification. In this context, diversification means you have a mix of both bullish positions and, to a smaller extent, bearish positions.

Indexes

ETFs that are bullish or bearish are ultimately tied to major market indexes. Take a quick look at indexes to better understand them (and the ETFs tied to them).

Whenever you hear the media commentary about "how the market is doing," it typically refers to a market proxy such as an index. You'll usually hear it mention "the Dow" or "the

S&P 500." There are other major market indexes, and there are many lesser, yet popular, measurements, such as the Dow Jones Transportation Average. Indexes and averages tend to be used interchangeably, but they're distinctly different entities.

Most people use these indexes basically as standards of market performance to see whether they're doing better or worse than a yardstick for comparison purposes. They want to know continuously whether their stocks, ETFs, mutual funds, or overall portfolios are performing well.

Great resources online, such as indexes.dowjones.com, give you the history and composition of indexes. For your purposes, these are the main ones to keep an eye on:

- **Dow Jones Industrial Average (DJIA):** This is the most widely watched index (technically it's not an index, but it's utilized as one). It tracks 30 widely owned, large cap stocks, and it's occasionally rebalanced to replace a stock that's not keeping up.

- **Nasdaq Composite:** This covers a cross section of stocks from Nasdaq. It's generally considered a mix of stocks that are high-growth (riskier) companies with an over-representation of technology stocks.

- **S&P 500 index:** This index tracks 500 leading, publicly traded companies considered to be widely held. The publishing firm Standard & Poor's created this index.

- **Wilshire 5000:** This index is considered the widest sampling of stocks across the general stock market and, therefore, a more accurate measure of stock market movement.

If you don't want to go nuts trying to "beat the market," consider an ETF that closely correlates to any of the indexes mentioned in the preceding list. Sometimes it's better to join 'em than to beat 'em. You can find ETFs that track or mirror the preceding indexes at sites such as www.etfdb.com.

9

Brokerage Orders and Trading Techniques

Investment success isn't just about *which* stocks to choose; it's also about *how* you choose those stocks. Frequently, investors think that good stock-picking means doing your homework and then making that buy (or sell). However, you can take it a step further to maximize profits (or minimize losses).

This chapter presents some of the best ways you can use powerful brokerage orders and trading techniques, which are useful whether you're buying or selling stock.

Brokerage Orders

Orders you place with your stockbroker fit neatly into three categories: time-related orders, condition-related orders, and advanced orders (such as trade triggers).

Get familiar with at least the first two types of orders, discussed in the following sections, because they're easy to implement, and they're invaluable tools for wealth-building and (more importantly) wealth-saving! Advanced orders usually are combinations of the first two types.

Speak with your broker about the different types of orders you can use to maximize the gains (or minimize the losses) from your stock investing. You also can read the broker's policies on stock orders at the brokerage website.

Time-related orders

A *time-related order* is just that — the order has a time limit. Typically, investors use these orders in conjunction with condition-related orders, described later in this chapter.

The two most common time-related orders are day orders and good-til-canceled (GTC) orders.

Day orders

A *day order* is an order to buy or sell a stock that expires at the end of that particular trading day. If you tell your broker, "Buy BYOB, Inc., at $37.50 and make it a day order," you mean that you want to purchase the stock at $37.50. But if the stock doesn't hit that price, your order expires, unfilled, at the end of the trading day.

When would you use day orders? It depends on your preferences and personal circumstances. I rarely use day orders because few events cause me to say, "I'll just try to buy or sell between now and the end of today's trading action." However, you may not want an order to linger beyond today's market action. Perhaps you want to test a price. ("I want to get rid of stock A at $39 to make a quick profit, but it's currently trading at $37.50. But I may change my mind tomorrow.") A day order is the perfect strategy to use in this case.

If you make a trade and don't specify a time limit with the order, most (if not all) brokers will automatically treat it as a day order.

Good-til-canceled orders

A *good-til-canceled (GTC) order* is the most commonly requested order by investors, and it's one that I use and recommend often. The GTC order stays in effect until it's transacted or until the investor cancels it. Although GTC orders are time-related, they're always tied to a condition, such as the stock achieving a certain price.

Most brokers have a limit of 30 or 60 days (or more). I've seen the limit as high as 120 days. By that time, either the broker cancels the order or contacts you to see whether you want to extend it. Ask your broker about his policy.

GTC orders are always coupled with condition-related orders (see the next section). Say that you think ASAP Corp. stock would make a good addition to your portfolio, but you don't want to buy it at the current price of $48 per share. You've done your homework on the stock, and you say, "This stock isn't worth $48 a share. I'd only buy it at $36 per share." (It's overpriced or overvalued according to your analysis.) Your best bet is to ask your broker to do a GTC order at $36. This request means that your broker will buy the shares if and when they hit the $36 mark (unless you cancel the order). Just make sure that your account has the funds available to complete the transaction.

GTC orders are useful, so become familiar with your broker's policy on them. While you're at it, ask whether any fees apply. Many brokers don't charge for GTC orders because if they happen to result in a buy (or sell) order, they generate a normal commission just as any stock transaction does. Other brokers may charge a small fee (but that's rare).

To be successful with GTC orders, you need to know

- **When you want to buy:** In recent years, people have had a tendency to rush into buying a stock without giving some thought to what they could do to get more for their money. Some investors don't realize that the stock market can be a place for bargain-hunting consumers. If you're ready to buy a quality pair of socks for $16 in a department store but the sales clerk says that those same socks are going on sale tomorrow for only $8, what do you do — assuming that you're a cost-conscious consumer? You probably decide to wait. The same point holds true with stocks.

   Say that you want to buy SOX, Inc., at $26, but it's currently trading at $30. You think that $30 is too expensive, but you'd be happy to buy the stock at $26 or lower. However, you have no idea whether the stock will move to your desired price today, tomorrow, next week, or even next month (or maybe never). In this case, a GTC order is appropriate.

- **When you want to sell:** What if you buy some socks at a department store and you discover that they have holes? Wouldn't you want to get rid of them? Of course you would. If a stock's price starts to unravel, you want to be able to get rid of it as well.

Perhaps you already own SOX at $25 but are concerned that market conditions may drive the price lower. You're not certain which way the stock will move in the future. In this case, a GTC order to sell the stock at a specified price is suitable. Because the stock price is $25, you may want to place a GTC order to sell it if it falls to $22.50 in order to prevent further losses. Again, GTC is the time frame, and it accompanies a condition (sell when the stock hits $22.50).

Condition-related orders

A *condition-related order* (also known as a *conditional order*) is executed only when a certain condition is met. Conditional orders enhance your ability to buy stocks at a lower price, to sell at a better price, or to minimize potential losses. When stock markets become bearish or uncertain, conditional orders are highly recommended.

A good example of a conditional order is a *limit order.* A limit order may say, "Buy Mojeski Corp. at $45." But if Mojeski Corp. isn't at $45 (this price is the condition), the order isn't executed. The following sections discuss limit orders, as well as market orders and stop-loss orders.

Market orders

When you buy stock, the simplest type of order is a *market order* — an order to buy or sell a stock at the market's current best available price. Here's an example: Kowalski, Inc., is available at the market price of $10. When you call your broker and instruct her to buy 100 shares "at the market," the broker implements the order for your account, and you pay $1,000 plus commission.

I say "current best available price" because the stock's price is constantly moving, and catching the best price can be a function of the broker's ability to process the stock purchase. For very active stocks, the price change can happen within seconds. It's not unheard of to have three brokers simultaneously place orders for the same stock and get three different prices because of differences in the brokers' capabilities.

The advantage of a market order is that the transaction is processed immediately, and you get your stock without worrying about whether it hits a particular price. For example, if you buy Kowalski, Inc., with a market order, you know that by the end of that phone call (or website visit), you're assured of getting the stock. The disadvantage of a market order is that you can't control the price at which you purchase the stock. Whether you're buying or selling your shares, you may not realize the exact price you expect.

Market orders get finalized in the chronological order in which they're placed. Your price may change because the orders ahead of you in line cause the stock price to rise or fall based on the latest news.

Stop-loss orders

A *stop-loss order* (also called a *stop order*) is a condition-related order that instructs the broker to sell a particular stock in your portfolio only when the stock reaches a particular price. It acts like a trigger, and the stop order converts to a market order to sell the stock immediately.

The stop-loss order isn't designed to take advantage of small, short-term moves in the stock's price. It's meant to help you protect the bulk of your money when the market turns against your stock investment in a sudden manner.

Say that your Kowalski, Inc., stock rises to $20 per share and you seek to protect your investment against a possible future market decline. A stop-loss order at $18 triggers your broker to sell the stock immediately if it falls to the $18 mark. In this example, if the stock suddenly drops to $17, it still triggers the stop-loss order, but the finalized sale price is $17. In a volatile market, you may not be able to sell at your precise stop-loss price. However, because the order automatically gets converted into a market order, the sale will be done, and you'll be spared further declines.

The main benefit of a stop-loss order is that it prevents a major loss in a stock that you own. It's a form of discipline that's important in investing to minimize potential losses. Investors can find it agonizing to sell a stock that has fallen. If they don't sell, however, the stock often continues to plummet as investors continue to hold on while hoping for a rebound in the price.

Most investors set a stop-loss amount at about 10 percent below the market value of the stock. This percentage gives the stock some room to fluctuate, which most stocks tend to do from day to day. If you're extra nervous, consider a tighter stop-loss, such as 5 percent or less.

Keep in mind that this order is a trigger, and a particular price isn't guaranteed to be captured because the actual buy or sell occurs immediately after the trigger is activated. If the market at the time of the actual transaction is particularly volatile, the price realized may be significantly different.

Trailing stops are an important technique in wealth preservation for seasoned stock investors and can be one of your key strategies in using stop-loss orders. A *trailing stop* is a stop-loss order that an investor actively manages by moving it up along with the stock's market price. The stop-loss order "trails" the stock price upward. As the stop-loss goes upward, it protects more and more of the stock's value from declining.

Say you bought stock in Peach, Inc. (PI) for $30 a share. A trailing stop is in place at 10 percent, and the order is GTC (with a time limit of 90 days for GTC orders). At $30 per share, the trailing stop is $27. If PI goes to $40, your trailing stop automatically rises to $36. If PI continues to rise to $50, your trailing continues along with it to $45. Now say that PI reverses course and starts to plummet. The trailing stop stays put at $45 and triggers a sell order if PI reaches the $45 level.

In the preceding example, I use a trailing stop percentage, but trailing stops are also available in dollar amounts. Say that PI is at $30, and I put in a trailing stop of $3. If PI rises to $50, my trailing stop will reach $47. If PI then drops from this peak of $50, the trailing stop stays put at $47 and triggers a sell order if PI actually hits $47.

William O'Neill, founder and publisher of *Investor's Business Daily*, advocates setting a trailing stop of 8 percent below your purchase price. That's his preference. Some investors who invest in very volatile stocks may put in trailing stops of 20 or 25 percent. Is a stop-loss order desirable or advisable in every situation? No. It depends on your level of experience, your investment goals, and the market environment. Still, stop-loss orders (trailing or otherwise) are appropriate in many cases, especially if the market seems uncertain (or you are!).

A trailing stop is a stop-loss order that you actively manage. The stop-loss order is good-til-canceled (GTC), and it constantly trails the stock's price as it moves up. To successfully implement stop-loss orders (including trailing stops), you should

- **Realize that brokers usually don't place trailing stops for you automatically.** In fact, they won't (or shouldn't) place any type of order without your consent. Deciding on the type of order to place is your responsibility.

- **Change the stop-loss order when the stock price moves significantly.** Change the stop-loss order when the stock price moves around 10 percent. For example, if you initially purchase a stock at $90 per share, ask the broker to place the stop-loss order at $81. When the stock moves to $100, cancel the $81 stop-loss order and replace it at $90. When the stock's price moves to $110, change the stop-loss order to $99, and so on.

- **Understand your broker's policy on GTC orders.** You don't want to risk a sudden drop in your stock's price without the stop-loss order protection. Note your broker's time limit so that you remember to renew the order for additional time.

- **Monitor your stock.** A trailing stop isn't a "set it and forget it" technique. Monitoring your investment is critical. Of course, if the investment falls, the stop-loss order prevents further loss. Should the stock price rise substantially, adjust your trailing stop accordingly. Keep raising the safety net as the stock continues to rise.

Limit orders

A *limit order* is a very precise condition-related order implying that a limit exists either on the buy or the sell side of the transaction. You want to buy (or sell) only at a specified price. Limit orders work well if you're buying the stock, but they may not be good for you if you're selling the stock. Here's how they work in both instances:

- **When you're buying:** Just because you like a particular company and you want its stock doesn't mean that you're willing to pay the current market price. Maybe you want to buy Kowalski, Inc., but the current market price of $20 per share isn't acceptable to you. You prefer to buy it at $16 because you think that price reflects its true market value. You tell your broker, "Buy Kowalski with a limit order at $16" (or you can enter a limit order at the broker's website). You have to specify whether it's a day order or a GTC order, which are discussed earlier in this chapter.

_____

_____

_____

What happens if the stock experiences great volatility? What if it drops to $16.01 and then suddenly drops to $15.95 on the next move? Nothing happens, actually, which you may be dismayed to hear. Because your order was limited to $16, it can be transacted only at $16 — no more and no less. The only way for this particular trade to occur is if the stock rises back to $16. However, if the price keeps dropping, then your limit order isn't transacted and may expire or be canceled.

- **When you're selling:** Limit orders are activated only when a stock hits a specific price. If you buy Kowalski, Inc., at $20 and you worry about a decline in the share price, you may decide to put in a limit order at $18. If you watch the news and hear that Kowalski's price is dropping, you may sigh and say, "I sure am glad I put in that limit order at $18." However, in a volatile market, the share price may leapfrog over your specified price. It could go from $18.01 to $17.99 and then continue its descent. Because the stock price never hit $18 on the mark, your stock isn't sold. You may be sitting at home satisfied (mistakenly) that you played it smart, while your stock plummets to $15, $10, or worse. Having a stop-loss order in place is best.

Investors who aren't in a hurry can use a limit order to try to get a better price when they decide to sell. For example, maybe you own a stock whose price is at $50 and you want to sell, but you think that a short-term rally in the stock is imminent. In that case, you can use a limit order such as, "Sell the stock at the sell limit order of $55 and keep the order on for 30 days."

When you're buying (or selling) a stock, most brokers interpret the limit order as "buy (or sell) at this specific price or better." For example, presumably, if your limit order is to buy a stock at $10, you'll be just as happy if your broker buys that stock at $9.95. That way, if you don't get exactly $10 because the stock's price was volatile, you'll still get the stock at a lower price. Talk to your broker to be clear on the meaning of the limit order.

Buy on Margin

Buying on margin means buying securities, such as stocks, with funds you borrow from your broker. Buying stock on margin is similar to buying a house with a mortgage. If you buy a

---

---

house at a purchase price of $100,000 and put 10 percent down, your equity (the part you own) is $10,000, and you borrow the remaining $90,000 with a mortgage. If the value of the house rises to $120,000 and you sell (for the sake of simplicity, I don't include closing costs in this example), you make a profit of 200 percent. How is that? The $20,000 gain on the property represents a gain of 20 percent on the purchase price of $100,000, but because your real investment is $10,000 (the down payment), your gain works out to 200 percent (a gain of $20,000 on your initial investment of $10,000).

Buying on margin is an example of using leverage to maximize your gain when prices rise. *Leverage* is using borrowed money when you make an asset purchase to increase your potential profit. This type of leverage is great in a favorable (bull) market, but it works against you in an unfavorable (bear) market. Say that a $100,000 house you purchase with a $90,000 mortgage falls in value to $80,000. Your outstanding debt of $90,000 exceeds the value of the property. Because you owe more than you own, you're left with a negative net worth.

Leverage is a double-edged sword. Don't forget that you need approval from your brokerage firm before you can buy on margin. To buy on margin, you typically fill out the form provided by that brokerage firm to be approved. Check with the broker because each firm has different requirements.

The following sections describe the potential outcomes of buying on margin, explain how to maintain a balance, and provide some pointers for successfully buying on margin.

Examine marginal outcomes

Suppose you think that the stock for the company Mergatroid, Inc., currently at $40 per share, will go up in value. You want to buy 100 shares, but you have only $2,000. What can you do? If you're intent on buying 100 shares (versus simply buying the 50 shares that you have cash for), you can borrow the additional $2,000 from your broker on margin. If you do that, what are the potential outcomes?

If the stock price goes up

This outcome is the best for you. If Mergatroid goes to $50 per share, your investment is worth $5,000, and your outstanding margin loan is $2,000. If you sell, the total proceeds will pay off the loan and leave you with $3,000. Because your initial investment was $2,000, your profit is a solid 50 percent because your $2,000 principal amount generated a $1,000 profit. (For the sake of this example, I leave out any charges, such as commissions and interest paid on the margin loan.) However, if you pay the entire $4,000 upfront without the margin loan, your $4,000 investment generates a profit of $1,000, or 25 percent. Using margin, you double the return on your money.

Leverage, when used properly, is very profitable. However, it's still debt, so understand that you must pay it off eventually, regardless of the stock's performance.

If the stock price fails to rise

If the stock goes nowhere, you still have to pay interest on that margin loan. If the stock pays dividends, this money can defray some of the margin loan's cost. In other words, dividends can help you pay off what you borrow from the broker. (Chapter 2 provides an introduction to dividends.)

Having the stock neither rise nor fall may seem like a neutral situation, but you pay interest on your margin loan with each passing day. For this reason, margin trading can be a good consideration for conservative investors if the stock pays a high dividend. Many times, a high dividend from 4,000 dollars' worth of stock can equal or exceed the margin interest you have to pay from the $2,000 (50 percent) you borrow from the broker to buy that stock.

If the stock price goes down, buying on margin can work against you. What if Mergatroid goes to $38 per share? The market value of 100 shares is then $3,800, but your equity shrinks to only $1,800 because you have to pay your $2,000 margin loan. You'd better be careful because the margin loan exceeds 50 percent of your stock investment. If it goes any lower, you may get a *margin call*, when the broker contacts you to ask you to restore the ratio between the margin loan and the value of the securities. See the following section for information about appropriate debt to equity ratios.

Maintain your balance

When you purchase stock on margin, you must maintain a balanced ratio of margin debt to equity of at least 50 percent. If the debt portion exceeds this limit, you're required to restore that ratio by depositing either more stock or more cash into your brokerage account. The additional stock you deposit can be stock that's transferred from another account.

To continue the example from the previous section: If Mergatroid goes to $28 per share, the margin loan portion exceeds 50 percent of the equity value in that stock — in this case, because the market value of your stock is $2,800 but the margin loan is still at $2,000, the margin loan is a worrisome 71 percent of the market value ($2,000 divided by $2,800 equals 71 percent). Expect to get a call from your broker to put more securities or cash into the account to restore the 50 percent balance.

If you can't come up with more stock, other securities, or cash, the next step is to sell stock from the account and use the proceeds to pay off the margin loan. That means you lose money on your investment.

The Federal Reserve Board governs margin requirements for brokers with Regulation T. Discuss this rule with your broker to understand fully your (and the broker's) risks and obligations. Regulation T dictates margin requirements set by brokers for their customers. For most listed stocks, it's 50 percent.

Strive for success on margin

Margin can escalate your profits on the up side but magnify your losses on the down side. If your stock plummets drastically, you can end up with a margin loan that exceeds the market value of the stock you used the loan to purchase.

_____

_____

_____

If you buy stock on margin, use a disciplined approach. Be extra careful when using leverage, such as a margin loan, because it can backfire. Keep the following points in mind:

- **Have ample reserves of cash or marginable securities in your account.** Try to keep the margin ratio at 40 percent or less to minimize the chance of a margin call.

  If you're a beginner, consider using margin to buy stocks in large companies that have relatively stable prices and pay good dividends. Some people buy income stocks that have dividend yields that exceed the margin interest rate, meaning that the stock ends up paying for its own margin loan. Just remember those stop-loss orders, discussed earlier in this chapter.

- **Constantly monitor your stocks.** If the market turns against you, the result will be especially painful if you use margin.

- **Have a payback plan for your margin debt.** Taking margin loans against your investments means that you're paying interest. Your ultimate goal is to make money, and paying interest eats into your profits.

_____

_____

_____

Go Short

The vast majority of stock investors are familiar with buying stock, holding on to it for a while, and hoping its value goes up. This kind of thinking is called *going long,* and investors who go long are considered to be *long on stocks.* Going long essentially means that you're bullish and seeking your profits from rising prices. However, astute investors also profit in the market when stock prices fall. *Going short* (also called *shorting a stock, selling short,* or *doing a short sale*) on a stock is a common technique for profiting from a stock price decline. Investors have made big profits during bear markets by going short. A short sale is a bet that a particular stock is going down.

Most people easily understand making money by going long. It boils down to "buy low and sell high." Going short means making money by selling high and then buying low. Consider an example that uses a fictitious company called DOA, Inc. As a stock, DOA ($50 per share) is looking pretty sickly. It has lots of debt and plummeting sales and earnings, and the news is out that DOA's industry will face hard times for the foreseeable future. This situation describes a stock that's an ideal candidate for shorting. The future may be bleak for DOA, but it's promising for savvy investors. The following sections provide the full scoop on going short.

You must understand brokerage rules before you conduct short selling. The broker must approve you for it (see Chapter 5 for information on working with brokers), and you must meet the minimum collateral requirement, which is typically $2,000 or 50 percent (whichever is higher) of the shorted stock's market value. If the stock generates dividends, those dividends are paid to the stock's owner, not to the person who borrows to go short. Check with your broker for complete details.

Because going short on stocks has greater risks than going long, I strongly advise beginning investors to avoid shorting stocks until they become more seasoned.

Set up a short sale

Say that you believe DOA is the right stock to short — you're pretty sure its price is going to fall. With DOA at $50, you instruct your broker to "go short 100 shares on DOA."

(It doesn't have to be 100 shares; I'm just using that as an example.) Here's what happens next:

1. **Your broker borrows 100 shares of DOA stock, either from his own inventory or from another client or broker.**

   The stock can be borrowed from a client, no permission necessary. The broker guarantees the transaction, and the client/stock owner never has to be informed about it because he never loses legal and beneficial right to the stock. You borrow 100 shares, and you'll return 100 shares when it's time to complete the transaction.

2. **Your broker then sells the stock and puts the money in your account.**

   Your account is credited with $5,000 (100 shares multiplied by $50) in cash — the money gained from selling the borrowed stock. This cash acts like a loan on which you're going to have to pay interest.

3. **You buy the stock back and return it to its rightful owner.**

When it's time to close the transaction (because either you want to close it or the owner of the shares wants to sell them, so you have to give them back), you must return the number of shares you borrowed (in this case, 100 shares). If you buy back the 100 shares at $40 per share (remember that you shorted this particular stock because you were sure its price was going to fall) and those 100 shares are returned to their owner, you make a $1,000 profit. (To keep the example tidy, I don't include brokerage commissions.)

Go short when prices grow taller

I bet you guessed that the wonderful profitability of selling short has a flip side. Say that you were wrong about DOA and that the stock price goes from $50 to $87. You still have to return the 100 shares you borrowed. With the stock's price at $87, that means you have to buy the stock for $8,700 (100 shares at the new, higher price of $87). How do you pay for it? Well, you have that original $5,000 in your account from when you initially went short on the stock. But where do you get the other $3,700 ($8,700 less the original $5,000)? You have to cough up the difference.

How much money do you lose if the stock goes to $100 or more? A heck of a lot. As a matter of fact, there's no limit to how much you can lose. That's why going short can be riskier than going long. When going long, the most you can lose is 100 percent of your money. When you go short, you can lose more than 100 percent of the money you invest.

Because the potential for loss is unlimited when you short a stock, use a stop order (also called a *buy-stop order*) to minimize the damage. Better yet, make it a good-til-canceled (GTC) order, discussed earlier in this chapter. You can set the stop order at a given price, and if the stock hits that price, you buy the stock back so that you can return it to its owner before the price rises even higher. You still lose money, but you limit your losses. Like a stop-loss order, a buy-stop order effectively works to limit your loss.

Going short can be a great maneuver in a declining (bear) market, but it can be brutal if the stock price goes up. If you're a beginner, stay away from short selling until you have enough experience (and money) to risk it.

10

Dealing with Taxes

After conquering the world of making money with stocks, now you have another hurdle — taxes. This chapter gives you the basics. *Note:* This chapter isn't meant to be comprehensive. For a fuller treatment of personal taxes, check with your personal tax advisor, and get the publications referenced in this chapter by either visiting the IRS website at www.irs.gov or calling the IRS publications department at 800-829-3676.

The Tax Treatment of Different Investments

The following sections tell you what you need to know about tax implications when you start investing in stocks.

Ordinary income and capital gains

Profit you make from your stock investments can be taxed in one of two ways, depending on the type of profit:

- **Ordinary income:** Your profit can be taxed at the same rate as wages — at your full, regular tax rate. If your tax bracket is 28 percent, for example, that's the rate at which your ordinary income investment profit is taxed. Two types of investment profits get taxed as ordinary income (check out IRS Publication 550, "Investment Income and Expenses," for more information): dividends and short-term capital gains.

  When you receive dividends (either in cash or stock), they're taxed as ordinary income. This is true even if those dividends are in a dividend reinvestment plan. If, however, the dividends occur in a tax-sheltered plan, such as an IRA or 401(k) plan, they're exempt from taxes for as long as they're in the plan. (Retirement plans are covered in the later section "Tax-Advantaged Retirement Investing.") Qualified dividends are taxed at a lower rate than nonqualified dividends. A *qualified dividend* is a dividend that receives preferential tax treatment versus other types of dividends.

If you sell stock for a gain and you've owned the stock for one year or less, the gain is considered ordinary income. To calculate the time, you use the *trade date* (or *date of execution*). This is the date on which you executed the order, not the settlement date. (For more on important dates, see Chapter 4.) However, if these gains occur in a tax-sheltered plan, such as a 401(k) or an IRA, no tax is triggered.

- **Long-term capital gains:** These are usually much better for you than ordinary income as far as taxes are concerned. The tax laws reward patient investors. After you've held the stock for at least a year and a day, your tax rate is reduced. Get more information on capital gains in IRS Publication 550.

Gains are taxable only if a sale actually takes place (in other words, only if the gain is "realized"). If your stock in GazillionBucks, Inc., goes from $5 per share to $87, that $82 appreciation isn't subject to taxation unless you actually sell the stock. Until you sell, that gain is "unrealized." Time your stock sales carefully and hold on to stocks for at least a year and a day (to make the gains long-term) to minimize the amount of taxes you have to pay on them.

When you buy stock, record the date of purchase and the *cost basis* (the purchase price of the stock plus any ancillary charges, such as commissions). This information is very important come tax time should you decide to sell your stock. The date of purchase (also known as the *date of execution*) helps establish the *holding period* (how long you own the stocks) that determines whether your gains are considered short-term or long-term.

Say you buy 100 shares of GazillionBucks, Inc., at $5 and pay a commission of $8. Your cost basis is $508 (100 shares times $5 plus $8 commission). If you sell the stock at $87 per share and pay a $12 commission, the total sale amount is $8,688 (100 shares times $87 less $12 commission). If this sale occurs less than a year after the purchase, it's a short-term gain. In the 28 percent tax bracket, the short-term gain of $8,180 ($8,688 minus $508) is also taxed at 28 percent. Read the following section to see the tax implications if your gain is a long-term gain.

Minimize the tax on your capital gains

Long-term capital gains are taxed at a more favorable rate than ordinary income. To qualify for long-term capital gains treatment, you must hold the investment for more than one year (in other words, for at least one year and one day).

Recall the example in the preceding section with GazillionBucks, Inc. As a short-term transaction at the 28 percent tax rate, the tax is $2,290 ($8,180 multiplied by 28 percent). You say, "What a chunk of dough. I better hold off a while longer." You hold on to the stock for more than a year to achieve the status of long-term capital gains. How does that change the tax? For anyone in the 28 percent tax bracket or higher, the long-term capital gains rate of 15 percent applies. In this case, the tax is $1,227 ($8,180 multiplied by 15 percent), resulting in a tax savings to you of $1,063 ($2,290 less $1,227). It's a substantial difference from the original tax.

Capital gains taxes *can* be lower than the tax on ordinary income, but they aren't higher. If, for example, you're in the 15 percent tax bracket for ordinary income and you have a long-term capital gain that would normally bump you up to the 28 percent tax bracket, the gain is taxed at your lower rate of 15 percent instead of a higher capital gains rate. Check with your tax advisor on a regular basis because this rule could change due to new tax laws.

Capital losses

Ever think that having the value of your stocks fall could be a good thing? Perhaps the only real positive regarding losses in your portfolio is that they can reduce your taxes. A *capital loss* means that you lost money on your investments. This amount is generally deductible on your tax return, and you can claim a loss on either long-term or short-term stock holdings. This loss can go against your other income and lower your overall tax.

Say you bought Worth Zilch Co. stock for a total purchase price of $3,500 and sold it later at a sale price of $800. Your tax-deductible capital loss is $2,700.

The one string attached to deducting investment losses on your tax return is that the most you can report in a single year is $3,000. On the bright side, though, any excess loss isn't really lost — you can carry it forward to the next year. If you have net investment losses of $4,500 in 2017, you can deduct $3,000 in 2017 and carry the remaining $1,500 loss over to 2018 and deduct it on your 2018 tax return.

Before you can deduct losses, you must first use them to offset any capital gains. If you realize long-term capital gains of $7,000 in Stock A and long-term capital losses of $6,000 in Stock B, you have a net long-term capital gain of $1,000 ($7,000 gain less the offset of $6,000 loss). See whether losses in your portfolio can be realized to offset any capital gains to reduce potential tax. IRS Publication 550 includes information for investors on capital gains and losses.

Where possible, keep losses on a short-term basis and push your gains into long-term capital gains status. If a transaction can't be tax-free, at the very least try to defer the tax to keep your money working for you.

Evaluate gains and losses scenarios

Any investor can come up possible gains and losses scenarios. For example, you may wonder what happens if you sell part of your holdings now as a short-term capital loss and the remainder later as a long-term capital gain. You must look at each sale of stock (or potential sale) to calculate the gain or loss you would realize from it. Figuring out your gain or loss isn't that complicated. Here are some general rules to help you. If you add up all your gains and losses and

- **The net result is a short-term gain:** It's taxed at your highest tax bracket (as ordinary income).

- **The net result is a long-term gain:** It's taxed at 15 percent if you're in the 28 percent tax bracket or higher. Check with your tax advisor on changes here.

- **The net result is a loss of $3,000 or less:** It's fully deductible against other income. If you're married filing separately, your deduction limit is $1,500.

- **The net result is a loss that exceeds $3,000:** You can deduct up to $3,000 in that year; the remainder goes forward to future years.

Share Gains with the IRS

You should buy or sell a stock because it makes economic sense first and consider the tax implications as secondary issues.

As long as you experience a *net gain* (gain after all transaction costs, including taxes, brokerage fees, and other fees), consider yourself a successful investor — even if you have to give away some of your gain to taxes.

Try to make tax planning second nature in your day-to-day activities. When you make a stock transaction, keep the receipt and maintain good records. When you make a large purchase or sale, ask yourself whether this transaction will have positive or negative tax consequences. (Refer to the earlier section "The Tax Treatment of Different Investments" to review various tax scenarios.) Speak to a tax consultant beforehand to discuss the ramifications.

The following sections describe the tax forms you need to fill out, as well as some important rules to follow.

Fill out forms

Most investors report their investment-related activities on their individual tax returns (Form 1040). The reports that you'll likely receive from brokers and other investment sources include the following:

- **Brokerage and bank statements:** Monthly statements that you receive
- **Trade confirmations:** Documents to confirm that you bought or sold stock
- **1099-DIV:** Reporting dividends paid to you
- **1099-INT:** Reporting interest paid to you
- **1099-B:** Reporting gross proceeds submitted to you from the sale of investments, such as stocks and mutual funds

 You may receive other, more obscure forms that aren't listed here. You should retain all documents related to your stock investments.

The IRS schedules and forms that most stock investors need to be aware of and/or attach to their Form 1040 include

- **Schedule B:** To report interest and dividends
- **Schedule D:** To report capital gains and losses

_____

_____

_____

- **Form 4952:** Investment Interest Expense Deduction
- **Publication 17:** Guide to Form 1040

You can get these publications directly from the IRS at 800-829-3676 or you can download them from the website (www.irs.gov). For more information on what records and documentation investors should hang on to, check out IRS Publication 552, "Recordkeeping for Individuals."

Play by the rules

Some people get the smart idea of "Hey! Why not sell my losing stock by December 31 to grab the short-term loss and just buy back the stock on January 2 so that I can have my cake and eat it, too?" The IRS puts the kibosh on maneuvers like that with something called the *wash-sale rule.* This rule states that if you sell a stock for a loss and buy it back within 30 days, the loss isn't valid because you didn't make any substantial investment change. The wash-sale rule applies only to losses. The way around the rule is simple: Wait at least 31 days before you buy that identical stock back again.

Some people try to get around the wash-sale rule by doubling up on their stock position with the intention of selling half. Therefore, the IRS makes the 30-day rule cover both sides of the sale date. That way, an investor can't buy the identical stock within 30 days just before the sale and then realize a short-term loss for tax purposes.

Tax Deductions for Investors

In the course of managing your stocks and other investments, you'll probably incur expenses that are tax-deductible. Tax laws allow you to write off certain investment-related expenses as itemized expenses on Schedule A, an attachment to IRS Form 1040. Keep records of your deductions and retain a checklist to remind you which deductions you normally take. IRS Publication 550 ("Investment Income and Expenses") gives you more details.

The following sections explain common tax deductions for investors. I also list a few items you *can't* deduct.

Investment interest

If you pay any interest to a stockbroker, such as margin interest or any interest to acquire a taxable financial investment, that's considered investment interest and is usually fully deductible as an itemized expense.

Keep in mind that not all interest is deductible. Consumer interest or interest paid for any consumer or personal purpose isn't deductible. For more general information, see the section covering interest in IRS Publication 17.

Miscellaneous expenses

Most investment-related deductions are reported as miscellaneous expenses. Here are some common deductions:

- Accounting or bookkeeping fees for keeping records of investment income
- Any expense related to tax service or education
- Computer expense — you can take a depreciation deduction for your computer if you use it 50 percent of the time or more for managing your investments
- Investment management or investment advisor's fees (fees paid for advice on tax-exempt investments aren't deductible)
- Legal fees involving stockholder issues

- Safe-deposit box rental fee or home safe to hold your securities, unless used to hold personal effects or tax-exempt securities
- Service charges for collecting interest and dividends
- Subscription fees for investment advisory services
- Travel costs to check investments or to confer with advisors regarding income-related investments

You can deduct only that portion of your miscellaneous expenses that exceeds 2 percent of your adjusted gross income. For more information on deducting miscellaneous expenses, check out IRS Publication 529.

Donations of stock to charity

What happens if you donate stock to your favorite (IRS-approved) charity? Because it's a noncash charitable contribution, you can deduct the market value of the stock.

Say that last year you bought stock for $2,000 and it's worth $4,000 this year. If you donate it this year, you can write off the market value at the time of the contribution. In this case, you have a $4,000 deduction. Use IRS Form 8283, which is an attachment to Schedule A, to report noncash contributions exceeding $500.

To get more guidance from the IRS on this matter, get Publication 526, "Charitable Contributions."

Items that you can't deduct

Here are some items you may think you can deduct but can't:

- Financial planning or investment seminars
- Any costs connected with attending stockholder meetings
- Home office expenses for managing your investments

Tax-Advantaged Retirement Investing

If you're going to invest for the long term (such as your retirement), you may as well maximize your use of tax-sheltered retirement plans. Many different types of plans are available;

the following sections touch on only the most popular ones. Although retirement plans may not seem relevant for investors who buy and sell stocks directly (as opposed to a mutual fund), some plans, called *self-directed retirement accounts,* allow you to invest directly.

IRAs

Individual Retirement Accounts (IRAs) are accounts you can open with a financial institution, such as a bank. An IRA is available to almost anyone who has earned income, and it allows you to set aside and invest money to help fund your retirement. Opening an IRA is easy, and virtually any bank or mutual fund can guide you through the process. Two basic types of IRAs are traditional and Roth.

Traditional IRA

The traditional Individual Retirement Account (also called the *deductible IRA*) was first popularized in the early 1980s. In a traditional IRA, you can make a tax-deductible contribution of up to $5,500 in 2017 (some restrictions apply). Individuals age 50 and older can make additional "catch-up" investments of $1,000. After 2017, the limits will be indexed to inflation.

The money can then grow in the IRA account unfettered by current taxes because the money isn't taxed until you take it out. You can start taking money out of your IRA in the year you turn 59½. The withdrawals at that point are taxed as ordinary income.

Keep in mind that you're required to start taking distributions from your account when you reach age 70½. After that point, you may no longer contribute to a traditional IRA. Again, check with your tax advisor to see how this criterion affects you personally.

If you take out money from an IRA too early, the amount is included in your taxable income, and you may be zapped with a 10 percent penalty. You can avoid the penalty if you have a good reason. The IRS provides a list of reasons in Publication 590-B, "Distributions from Individual Retirement Arrangements (IRAs)."

To put money into an IRA, you must earn income equal to or greater than the amount you're contributing. *Earned income* is money made either as an employee or a self-employed person. Although traditional IRAs can be great for investors, the toughest part about them is qualifying — they have income limitations and other qualifiers that make them less deductible based on how high your income is. See IRS Publication 590-A, "Contributions to Individual Retirement Arrangements (IRAs)," for more details.

 Stock investors can open a self-directed IRA with a brokerage firm. This means that you can buy and sell stocks in the account with no taxes on dividends or capital gains. The account is tax-deferred, so you don't have to worry about taxes until you start making withdrawals.

Roth IRA

Here are some ways to distinguish the Roth IRA from the traditional IRA:

- The Roth IRA provides no tax deduction for contributions.

- Money in the Roth IRA grows tax-free and can be withdrawn tax-free when you turn 59½.

- The Roth IRA is subject to early distribution penalties (although there are exceptions). Distributions have to be qualified to be penalty- and tax-free; in other words, make sure that any distribution is within the guidelines set by the IRS (see Publication 590-B).

The maximum contribution per year for Roth IRAs is the same as for traditional IRAs. You can open a self-directed account with a broker as well. See IRS Publication 590-A for details on qualifying.

401(k) plans

Company-sponsored 401(k) plans are widely used and very popular. In a 401(k) plan, companies set aside money from their employees' paychecks that employees can use to invest for retirement. Generally, in 2017 you can invest as much as $18,000 of your pretax earned income and have it grow tax-deferred. Those over age 50 can contribute more as a "catch-up" contribution.

Usually, the money is put in mutual funds administered through a mutual fund company or an insurance firm. Although most 401(k) plans aren't self-directed, I mention them in this book for good reason.

Because your money is in a mutual fund that may invest in stocks, take an active role in finding out the mutual funds in which you're allowed to invest. Most plans offer several types of stock mutual funds. Use your growing knowledge about stocks to make more informed choices about your 401(k) plan options. For more information on 401(k) and other retirement plans, check out IRS Publication 560.

About the Author

Paul Mladjenovic is a Certified Financial Planner (CFP), a national seminar leader, an author, and a consultant. Since 1981, he has specialized in investing, financial planning, and home business issues. During those 30-plus years, he has helped thousands of students and readers build wealth through his nationwide seminars, workshops, conferences, and coaching program.

Paul is the author of *Stock Investing For Dummies, High-Level Investing For Dummies, Micro-Entrepreneurship For Dummies, Zero-Cost Marketing, Precious Metals Investing For Dummies*, and *The Job Hunter's Encyclopedia*. His national (and online) seminars include "The $50 Wealth-Builder," "Ultra-Investing with Options," and the "Home Business Goldmine," among others. The full details on his (downloadable) financial and business startup audio seminars can be found at www.RavingCapitalist.com.

Since 2000, Paul has built a reputation as an accurate economics and market forecaster. His long record includes accurate forecasts of the housing bubble, the energy crisis, the Great Recession, the rise of precious metals, and much more. He has been interviewed or referenced by numerous media sources, such as Comcast, CNN, MarketWatch, Bloomberg, Fox Business, *Futures* magazine, GoldSeek.com, PreciousMetalsInvesting.com, Minyanville.com, and FinancialSense.com.

You can view Paul's profile at www.linkedin.com/in/paulmladjenovic/ and follow him at www.twitter.com/paulmlad. Readers can email questions or inquiries directly at paul@mladjenovic.com or through the contact page at www.RavingCapitalist.com.